Children and Conversion

Children
and
Conversion

Edited by Clifford Ingle

BROADMAN PRESS
Nashville, Tennessee

Dewey Decimal Classification Number: 234
Library of Congress Catalog Card Number: 79-113212
Printed in the United States of America
4.O6914

To John Barry and Thomas Lynn
with a father and mother's prayer

Preface

This book is an outgrowth of a paper entitled "Guidelines for a Theology of Children," which was presented at the fall convocation of Midwestern Baptist Theological Seminary in 1965. Two and one-half years' research involved professors in the biblical, theological, and educational fields of the six Southern Baptist seminaries, professors in the fields of education and psychology of numerous universities, children's workers of the Southern Baptist Sunday School Board, and numerous pastors and ministers of education of Baptist churches. Most of these read the paper after its completion. Many of them, along with others who had heard it presented or who had read it, suggested that it be developed into a book.

Thus it was with high hopes of making a timely contribution to the Baptist people who have educated me and given me opportunities for service that the project was begun. But the aspiring author soon realized that only a symposium could begin to do justice to so broad and profound a subject. Although multiple authorship must sacrifice a certain amount of unity, it provides at least two compensating values. First, it takes advantage of the variety of personality, specialized training, and experience of men in several fields of study. Second, the subject is approached from a wider and more balanced perspective than any one author could provide. An attempt was made to utilize to the fullest the insights of all contributors by submitting to them the first draft of each chapter for critical evaluation and suggestions before the final draft was written.

7

All of us who have worked on the book hope the reader will remember that this is a pioneer work. Many Baptists have been giving serious thought to the relation of children to the church, and some have written and spoken on various aspects of the subject, G. R. Beasley-Murray having done more than anyone else. Yet as far as can be ascertained, this is the first work of its kind to be produced by Baptists. It is only a beginning and certainly will not meet the needs of all readers.

No one book can appeal adequately to the variety of academic levels which exist among members of Baptist churches; so no one book can provide the variety of levels on which the subject matter needs to be treated. Also, most of the areas to which a chapter has been devoted in this book could well be book-length treatments. The answers which we have tried to give to many questions are far from adequate, and there are many important questions which have not been treated at all. This subject needs the fullest and best development which Baptist people can give it, and we look with hope toward other denominations to make meaningful contributions to this area of common need.

The editor wishes to express here his appreciation to each writer who has shared in this work. To the large number of professors, children's workers, pastors, and ministers of education who have contributed both materials and invaluable suggestions, we give our thanks. A debt of gratitude is expressed to Vera (Mrs. James G.) Rice for the typing of the manuscripts, and to my wife, who as a scholar in her own right and a teacher in a public elementary school, has given valuable insights and encouragement.

A special debt of gratitude is expressed to Dr. Millard J. Berquist, president of Midwestern Baptist Theological Seminary, and to the Seminary's trustees for providing such excellent facilities and an atmosphere which encourages research and writing.

CONTENTS

I

Why the Interest?
Clifford Ingle

The Confusion Among Us

There are differences of opinion among us which point to a need for an adequate theology of children. The following illustrations make this quite clear: A pastor heard the director of the preschool department (ages 0-6) teaching the little children to repeat the Lord's Prayer. He entered the room and interrupting the superintendent, said: "You must not teach them to pray 'Our Father,' for God is not their father; they are of their father the devil."

A seminary professor's wife, serving as a public school counselor, called me and said: "I need help. My youngest child has wanted to become a Christian ever since she was five (now six). I thought I knew all the answers, but I must confess I am not so sure anymore. Is it actually possible for a six-year-old child to be saved?"

According to one Baptist theologian, no person is intellectually capable of making a responsible decision to become a Christian until he is around fifteen or sixteen years of age.

A Baptist mother said: "I am the chairman of the local branch of the National Organization for Child Evangelism. I believe little children as early as four may make a simple trust in Jesus. Remember, Jesus said, 'Unless you become as a little child.' "

During the invitation at the close of a Sunday worship service, a pastor saw his seventeen-year-old son come forward. The father said later that he thought his son was coming for special service since the boy had been a Christian since he was nine years of age. But the son had said: "Dad, I'm accepting Christ as my Saviour. I now realize

11

that I did not know what I was doing when I joined the church at nine."

A religious psychologist states that children under twelve years of age who are accepted into Southern Baptist churches have received only *infant baptism*. He consistently refuses to vote to receive for church membership anyone under twelve years of age. Yet one of his children accepted Christ and was received for baptism and church membership before the age of twelve. When questioned about this inconsistency, he replied that his child's case was different; for she had received careful instruction and knew what she was doing.

Personal research continues to reveal some remarkable incongruities among Southern Baptists. Many individuals contend that it is practically impossible for a child under twelve or thirteen years of age to have reached the mental, emotional, or spiritual maturity which is necessary for experiencing a genuine repentance for sin and submission to Christ as Saviour and Lord. Yet when questioned concerning their children, practically everyone said that decisions to become a Christian were made by their children before the age of twelve. The defense was that they were carefully instructed and so knew what they were doing.

One could easily multiply illustrations which would further point up the confusion among us concerning the status and place of children in relation to Christ and his church.

A Direction of Concern

The interest as well as confusion is not limited to Southern Baptists. During and following World War II, the place of children in relation to Christ and the church became a subject of lively discussion by leaders of most denominations in both the Americas and Europe. In *The Teaching of the Church Regarding Baptism,* Karl Barth questions the validity of infant baptism and insists that "children . . . are in the kingdom . . . but not in the church, and that parents ought to know this."

In November, 1963, the Baptist Union Council of the British Isles appointed a study group to prepare a paper on the Baptist view of the relation of the child to the church. The following reasons for this study were given: (1) to formulate a basis for denominational policy in respect to children and young people; (2) to contribute to the current ecumenical discussion of Christian initiation, nurture, and the meaning of the church. The findings were published in a booklet which is available to the public, *The Child and Church,* by the Carey Kingsgate Press, 6 Southampton Row, London, W.C.I.

The editors of the journal of *Religious Education,* a national publication, gave the major part of the September-October issue (1963) to a symposium on "The Proper Age for a Declaration of Faith." The response to the symposium was so great that it led to a follow-up series of articles. These appeared in the July-August issue (1965).

A bishop of the Methodist church addressing a Southern Baptist Seminary meeting said that he was of the conviction that infant baptism has no scriptural basis and should be abandoned. He added that his position on this matter was well known among his own people.

Perhaps Simon Doniger best perceives the subject when he says, "Even now we are only at the beginning of developing a proper Christian theology of the child or a 'doctrine of the child' that has lost all traces of being merely a watered-down adulthood."

A Closer Look

Research on the subject of the child and his place in Southern Baptist church life has revealed several things. First, no work could be found by a Baptist theologian that dealt extensively with matters which are essential to the subject, such as the nature of a newborn child—is he a child of God or a child of wrath or neither? What is meant by becoming accountable to God? What are the minimal requirements to begin life as a Christian?

Second, there is a paradox between the educational curricula of Southern Baptist churches and the content of our worship services. In the services of worship the children hear the language of sin and salvation in adult terminology. Yet there is the strong probability that few of them have been prepared to understand the words and concepts. Specifically, if a small child is presented with the fearful prospects of an endless hell of fire (and damnation) and told that going before the group and saying "I love Jesus" will eliminate the danger, can we say that his doing so indicates any degree of spiritual insight? Since this has occurred, especially during revival meeetings, the advisability of taking small children to such meetings is questionable.

The manner in which many worship and revival services are presently conducted place the writers of children's educational materials in a most difficult position. Either we must assume that children of five or six years of age have the ability to grasp the essential spiritual concepts of Christian conversion and instruct the writers of children's materials accordingly, or we need to examine more carefully what is being done in our services.

Third, an increasing number of children below the ages of nine are being received for membership in Southern Baptist churches; yet according to available figures, the dropouts from active church participation is higher during the years of fifteen to nineteen than at any other time. While many things may contribute to this situation, we cannot escape the possibility of a direct relationship between early acceptance into church membership and dropouts. We have many reasons to question the degree of insight with which a declaration of faith is made by those under nine or ten years of age.

Fourth, according to surveys, the average age of baptism among Southern Baptists has steadily dropped during the twentieth century. (1) From 1899 to 1916, the average age for conversion and church membership was sixteen. Conversion, baptism, and church membership were considered to be adult experiences. This was in sharp contrast with the churches who were practicing infant baptism. (2) Following World War I, the receiving of children for conversion and church membership was gradually lowered until the age of twelve.

(3) From about 1935 to 1955, the norm for conversion came to be nine to ten years. To wait until beyond twelve was considered to be dangerous. (4) During the years since 1955, efforts are being made to evangelize the preschool child. This is to be witnessed especially during Vacation Bible School and revival meetings. According to the 1966-67 reports of Southern Baptist churches, *Quarterly Review,* October-December, 1967, pp. 22-31, the distribution of baptisms according to age are as follows:

Under 6	1,146
6-8 years old	34,026
9-12 years old	139,211
13-16 years old	59,569
17-24 years old	46,980
25 or older	80,027
	360,959

On the basis of this trend, it is reasonable to expect that children of four and five years of age will be considered as prospects for evangelistic activity.

The question may be rightly asked, "Why has our church leadership permitted these trends to go unchecked?" Dr. William Hull, professor of New Testament at Southern Baptist Theological Seminary, suggests two basic reasons:

First, it is relatively easy to direct the very young to apply for church membership. The overly zealous parent, teacher, or pastor may exploit the child's simple trust.

Second, most Baptists, according to Hull, have failed to develop an adequate theology for children. They have limited their understanding of salvation exclusively to a conversion (immediate experience) theology developed by and for adults. This means that the only invitation to which a child can respond is "repent and be saved." Since this is the "way it is done," this is accepted by the child and the church, as being the only response he can make, and to such a response most church members give automatic approval.

One cannot help wondering about the nature of the experience undergone when a child can only nod assent to such questions as, "You know Jesus died for your sins?" "You are confessing your sins and feel Jesus has saved you?" This is not to question these decisions being made later in life. It is to question the ability of a child to understand and accept salvation in its New Testament dimensions.

What Southern Baptists need is a positive theological understanding of the child and of the religious reality to which he may appropriately respond.

Some Basic Terms

Some terms may be profitably clarified to insure a meeting of minds between the writers and the readers.

First, the word "theology" is composed of two Greek words *theos* —God, and *logos*—a reasoned study or expression. Thus theology is a reasoned study or expression of the relation of a thing(s) or person(s) to God. For example, one may speak of a theology of evangelism, of possessions, of missions, of work and leisure. The formation and expression of theology are not limited to the Bible itself, for theology may treat God's relationship with anything or anyone in time and space. Thus it is quite proper to speak of a theology of the child and the church, as the subject of this book is the relationship between the child and the church under God.

Second, any attempt to formulate a theology of the child and the church must come to grips with the most difficult question, "Who" (what) is a child? Any Christian answer must take into account the understanding of God, the universe, and selfhood as expressed by Old Testament writers.

The people of God in the Old Testament came to an understanding of God as he revealed himself to them through his activity among them. The outstanding activity or event was God's delivering them from Egyptian bondage, guiding them through the wilderness into the land which he had promised them, and his continuing acts of judgment and mercy upon them.

Thus, God was seen first as "deliverer" (redeemer). Seeing his power over men and the forces of nature in this experience, led them to the conviction that God was also the supreme Creator and controller of all things. For this reason the entire Bible is marked by the continuing theme, that the God of Israel is the supreme Creator and Redeemer, and that the universe is an instrument (tool) through which he accomplishes his purpose. Therefore, we are to recognize that the universe (man included) was created to glorify and serve God.

The reason the Israelite could get along with one God, while other religions of the time had many, was that his one God was sufficient to give meaning to everything. Since God was one, everything created by him possessed oneness, was a unity. Because Old Testament people considered man to be created in God's image, man must also be a true unity.

One of the wholesome current theological trends is the growing recognition that the Bible pictures man as a unity of flesh and spirit rather than as a combination of two unrelated parts, spirit (soul)— matter (body). This emphasizes the fact that any attempt to understand a child in biblical terms must recognize that the biological, psychological, sociological, and intellectual aspects are only differing ways of considering a unified being.

Herein leaders in the various fields of child study may be just as guilty of failing to see the unity of the whole person as have students of the Bible. For example, the physiologist may see the child only as a functioning animal possessing certain structural and functional potentials for growth. The educator may view the child as a creature possessing certain learning processes. The psychologist may see him as a personality structure experiencing the development of the id, ego, and superego. The theologian may define a child as a soul formed by a body. Yet, a child is all these and more! He is a living person in physical form.

So any approach which fails to see the child as a unity—a self—is falling short of the biblical concept of man. Therefore, adequate biological, sociological, psychological, and spiritual insights are needed to understand the child in each stage of his development.

A major difficulty to be faced is that the Bible tells us nothing about the nature and status of a child. It does give views of man by the variety of words used in referring to him (see chaps. 2 and 6). One example will be sufficient for our purpose. Scholars of the Hebrew and Greek languages state that the word translated as "soul" is more accurately translated as "self." A child is a person, a self composed of flesh and spirit with all the potentials which all of these possess. So each self has form and structure. This must be seen as God's gift of life.

Whatever else may be said concerning an infant, the following seems to be in keeping with the Scriptures: at birth each child is a self —a person. Being made in God's image, he has the potential for responding to God. At the same time there is at the heart of human nature the potential for rejecting God through the committing of active wrongs. Thus from the beginning of his life every person is marked by the presence of potential conflict which stems from his inmost nature. Thus each is dependent upon the power of divine grace to give direction to the redemption of his life.

The third word needing clarification is church. Any attempt to give one simple, all-inclusive definition is doomed to failure. The writers of the New Testament made no such effort. Also, with the passing of time the variety of meanings applied to the word "church" was multiplied, not lessened.

The term is used to designate all of Christ's followers. It is used to refer to a particular group, such as a denomination, "the Methodist Church." It is used to refer to a local congregation. It is frequently used to designate Christianity as an ecclesiastical power, "the church hierarchy." An increasingly frequent practice is to use the term to refer to any specific religion, "the Jewish church." Perhaps the most common usage is to designate a building at a certain location, or the meetings of certain congregations as church. Too, contemporary Christianity is so devoted to organizational and institutional matters that it is difficult for most Christians to understand the New Testament teaching that Christ's church is wherever his followers are gathered (Matt. 18:20).

The simple fact is that when attempts are made to define "church" to mean some kind of religious organization and structure, every group from the most highly organized (Roman Catholic) to the least organized (Quakers) can find scriptural proof texts to show the correctness of its particular structure. This would certainly indicate that no one group can use the entire New Testament to justify its claim to be the "one true church" from which all other groups have become separated. Baptists have as much right to refer to the Roman Catholic Church as "separated from us" as Pope John XXIII had to refer to Protestants as "our separated brethren." According to the New Testament, both ideas are in error.

One thing is evident concerning Christ's followers in the New Testament. They believed that God in Christ had established a new people (new covenant, new community), and each congregation was an embodiment of that covenant relationship. These were not thought of primarily as organized bodies but as communities which were formed and bound together by the Spirit. The New Testament suggests that each community was a member of Christ's entire body (1 Thess. 1:1; 2:14).

The concept of the church as a local congregation (Rom. 16:5; Col. 4:15); as all the people of God in a city and its vicinity (Acts 5:11); as including one or more provinces (Acts 9:31); and as the body of Christ composed of all true believers, past, present, and future (Eph. 1:22-23; 5:21-33) is in the New Testament.

Any attempted definition of "church" must include its mission as well as its constituents (body). It is never adequate to say the church is only a fellowship of believers. It is a fellowship of believers called by its Lord into a ministry of reconciliation—a perpetual evangelistic endeavor. In being true to its nature, the church is at its center a fellowship of believers surrounded by a countless number of children, young people, and adults who are at varying stages of reaction to the gospel. They share in the worship, are the recipients of the church's teaching, and are in a mingled fellowship "with" believers but are not "of" the fellowship of believers.

To be more specific: A church provides opportunities for those learning and worshipping experiences through which its members grow toward Christian maturity. It must also provide adequate Christian nurture for little children which will prepare them for the time when they, as responsible persons, will be faced with the choice of accepting or rejecting Christ. To do less would be a rejection of the church's mission.

Thus the church must live and act in the constant tension of being a community of the Spirit and of leading others into the community through Christ.

For our purposes "church" will be used to refer to a local congregation. Ultimately it is only as one labors in and through a specific congregation that meaning is given to any New Testament concept of the church.

2

The Child Within the Old Testament Community
Roy L. Honeycutt, Jr.

A few places in the Old Testament indicate that children, at least at times, attended public forms of worship. These, however, do not tell us how old such children were or what may have been involved in deciding when a child should be recognized as a full-fledged member of the worshiping community.

Within the legal sections of the Old Testament, there is a total absence of provisions about admitting children to full religious status. This is important, for the religious system carefully spelled out details about many other matters. The absence of rules in this area implies that, except for circumcision, children were accepted without going through any ritual or meeting any other requirements.

Passages Showing the Relation of the Child

Circumcision was very important in the Old Testament. It was the symbol which identified members of the covenant community (cf. Gen. 17:9ff; 34:14-16; Ex. 12:47-48). It was given a uniquely religious interpretation and was performed on the eighth day after birth (cf. Lev. 12:3; Gen. 17:12). Thus, one can hardly fail to conclude that the male infant was reckoned to have been a full member of the covenant community. The Old Testament refers to no further ceremony or rite beyond circumcision which marked the person as a full covenant member.

There are legal passages within the Old Testament which call for the dedication of the first-born son at infancy (cf. Ex. 22:29b-30;

34:19-20; 13:1-2; 13:14-15; Deut. 15:19-20; Num. 18:15-18; 3:47). Not only is the first-born son dedicated to the Lord, but through the single act of dedicating the first-born son all childen to follow were also dedicated. There is no evidence that succeeding children of a marriage were dedicated to the Lord. Their dedication was already effected through the dedication of the first-born male.

Dedication of the first-born male child did not involve dedication in the sense that one outside the covenant now entered into covenant faith. Primarily it illustrated the manner in which all of creation belongs to God—especially those within the covenant, including their offspring. Children born into a family were already God's special possession. The ceremony of dedication publicly recognized an already established relationship. In paying the redemption price (Num. 18:15f), the father acknowledged that the first-born son and all future offspring actually belonged to the Lord, and were entrusted to man through God's grace.

Narratives which describe the dedication of the child at infancy or extremely early years are instructive. Samson was dedicated to the Lord from birth (cf. Judg. 13:5,7), and it is generally assumed that Nazirites other than Samson might also be dedicated to God "from birth to the day of his death" (Judg. 13:7). The Nazirite vow could also be for less than life-long duration, however, and might be assumed later in life than infancy (cf. Num. 6:1ff).

A well-known story concerning the dedication of a child to the Lord concerns Samuel (1 Sam. 1:24f). The biblical text states only that "the child was young" and that he was dedicated after his mother weaned him. While there is no basis for assuming that this was the normal pattern, this is nonetheless a clear example of a child hardly beyond infancy who was taken to the shrine and dedicated to the Lord.

There is an experience later in the life of Samuel that is illuminating, however, and may shed light on the volitional and experiential relationship between Samuel and the Lord. Ministering in the temple at Shiloh with Eli (cf. 1 Sam. 3:3), Samuel heard someone calling. Believing it to be Eli, he answered the priest. Eli finally understood that it was the Lord who in some way was impressing himself upon Samuel, and advised Samuel, saying, "Go, lie down; and if he calls you, you shall say, 'Speak, Lord, for thy servant hears'" (1 Sam. 3:9). Most instructive however, is the explanation inserted in the midst of the narrative, "Now Samuel did not yet know the Lord, and the word of the Lord had not yet been revealed to him" (1 Sam. 3:7).

Here is the only example, within the Old Testament, so far as I am aware, in which an individual is described as apparently having come to know the Lord after having been dedicated to his service for a previous period of time. It is impossible to determine Samuel's age at the time, but he was sufficiently old as to be described as "ministering to the Lord under Eli" (1 Sam. 3:1).

The Samuel narrative reveals two significant points. First, an individual could be dedicated to the Lord from infancy, and thus included within the broader circle of religious structures. Second, however, such an individual could have a new or special kind of experience—"Samuel did not yet know the Lord."

The narrative concerning the death of the first child of David and Bathsheba is instructive with regard to the manner in which an infant was identified as a permanent part of the covenant community (cf. 2 Sam. 12:15ff). Briefly stated, David prayed and fasted during the child's illness, but following his death he resumed his normal activities. Perplexed concerning this, David's servants asked for an explanation. David concluded his explanation by saying, "Why should I fast? Can I bring him back again? I shall go to him, but he will not return to me" (2 Sam. 12:23).

Whatever one's views concerning Israelite beliefs on life after death (and there are many divergent views today), whether David and the child faced continued union in a common family grave, in Sheol, or however one may understand existence beyond death, the point is that David's comfort rested in the indissoluble union of himself and the child. The father and the child shared in a union, a "oneness," which could not be broken. Once one enters into the family circle that bond is never shattered; not even by death.

Hence, one's union within the covenant family is both real and indissoluble. It is so not because of one's volitional commitment but simply because one has been born into covenant existence. Whatever one may conclude about the nature of David's understanding of his union with the child, there was an indissoluble union within the covenant family that not even death could shatter.

Under the leadership of the priest Jehoiada, Joash was delivered and later crowned king at the age of seven (cf. 2 KINGS 11:4ff, 21). Although Jehoiada was the force behind the throne, the fact that a seven-year-old served as king is significant for understanding the role of children in the community of faith. The office of king was not only political, but had specifically religious overtones in which the king played a vital part. Admittedly, the fact that a seven-year-old boy served as king under the direction of a wise priest does not "prove" that children normally participated in public affairs of worship, to say nothing of affairs of state. But it does show that Joash was an accepted part of the covenant community. He was so not because of any volitional decision or commitment, but because he had been born into the covenant family.

In summary, each of the five narratives illustrates the manner in which children, some in infancy, were considered part of the community of faith. This involved no decision on their own part, so far as can be discerned. The most probable conclusion is that the child was viewed as part of the community of faith simply by virtue of having been born into the "household of faith."

The Covenant and Corporate Solidarity

How were infants assumed to have been within the Israelite covenant? Why was there no apparent time of personal decision when an Israelite youth committed himself to the faith of Israel? Why was there no concern for the relationship between age and the participation of the child in formal religious affairs? There are two concepts, to a great extent unique with Israel, which form the foundation from which these questions may be answered.

First, the concept of the covenant is fundamental to an understanding of the relationship of the child to the worshipping community.

The covenant was the fundamental religious concept for Old Testament faith. Although numerous covenants are mentioned within the Old Testament, the fundamental covenant for the nation at large was the covenant at Sinai. The essence of the covenant relationship is summarized in the assertion that the Lord will be their God and Israel will be his people (cf. Ex. 6:7; Hos. 2:23; Jer. 31:33). It was upon the foundation of the covenant that Israel emerged as a religious people. Thus, the covenant community of the Old Testament is a direct parallel to the church in the New Testament.

1. The inclusive nature of the covenant.—All of life was embraced by the covenant. If one was part of the covenant community he was part of the whole of that community; family, work, recreation, "church," the entirety of life. Thus, a child born into a covenant family was part of the whole of the covenant community. He did not live in a noncovenantal area of existence and later decide to enter the covenant community. When a child came into the world, he came into the fulness of the covenant community; a community that embraced every aspect of life, including the worshipping community.

Too often we today have a divided concept of church and community which leads to the idea that when one "joins the church" he moves from one segment of society to another, that he leaps a great wall which forever stands dividing life into covenant and noncovenant, sacred and secular.

2. The covenant originated in and was maintained with collective groups.—A brief reading of Exodus 24:1ff reveals that the covenant was made with Israel as a corporate body. When one considers the singular form of address used in the Ten Commandments, it is obvious that there were individual responsibilities within that corporate bond. We also see the manner in which individuals are continually held responsible throughout the Old Testament for matters of ethical and ritual conduct of a personal nature. Thus, "all Israel" were covenant members. The adult male member shared in the covenant made with collective Israel, and the members of his family shared in the covenant because of the father-husband's participation in the covenant.

3. The perpetuity of the covenant.—Was the covenant automatic or did it have to be reaffirmed by every individual? To this question there is both a qualified "yes" and "no." The covenant was automatic in that every individual was born into the covenant community, a community of faith, as infant circumcision should clearly indicate.

Thus, no member of the covenant community ever faced the decision of whether he would enter the community of faith. He was already part of the covenant of faith. The covenant offered no right of termination to either God or Israel. God had already declared that he would never terminate the covenant, and should Israel terminate it she would do so not because of its terms of agreement but because she had acted dishonorably. In this sense the covenant was perpetual.

On the other hand, the covenant was not automatic in the sense that every generation remained within the covenant regardless of its faithfulness to covenant obligations.

H. H. Rowley observes, "Israel's election was not something automatic that made her his people for all time by mere physical generation. She entered into the covenant voluntarily, and each generation must renew it by accepting for itself its obligations, or it would place itself outside the covenant."

But how was the covenant renewed? Probably, each new generation renewed the covenant by (1) participation in a group covenant renewal ceremony during which the motifs of redemption (Exodus events), law (the Ten Commandments), and creation (elements of the creation narratives), were interwoven in a living and present re-creation of God's wondrous acts for his people, (2) by individual manifestation of personal character consonant with the demands of covenant relationship (cf. the declaratory oaths of Psalm 15, 24; Isa. 33; Ezek. 18:5ff; Job 31:1ff), and (3) by sharing in the family celebration of Passover.

Thus, the only decision an individual ever faced within Israel was whether or not he would remain within the covenant, not whether he would enter the covenant, or share in the worshipping community. He, and the community with him, was already within the covenant faith. God had promised this for all ages. One's only decision was whether he would remain within the faith community.

Therefore issues concerning the child and the church, especially with regard to conversion and the "age of accountability," would have been inconceivable to Old Testament thought.

Second, the principle of corporate solidarity is fundamental to an understanding of the relationship between the child and the community of faith. This principle does more than any other single emphasis to explain how an infant could be conceived, apart from personal decision, as part of the faith community.

Social solidarity is found among all primitive but socially organized groups, and Robinson suggests that no one should overlook the concept of corporate personality within the Old Testament. As he indicates, there are many examples in the Old Testament in which the total family or clan is summed up in one person, the one acting on behalf of or involving the whole in his action.

Just as Achan's disobedience brought about the defeat of the larger group, a defeat ascribed to having offended God, so his subsequent judgment also involved the destruction of his entire family: "And Joshua and all Israel with him took Achan the son of Zerah, . . . and his sons and daughters, and his oxen and asses and sheep, and his tent, and all that he had . . . And all Israel stoned him with stones; they burned them with fire, and stoned them with stones . . . Therefore that place is called, the Valley of Achor" (Josh. 7:24-26).

All of the family was summed up in Achan. His sin was shared by the family group, just as his judgment was experienced by the whole of the family.

With regard to the present issue of the child and the church, all of this comes into focus in the centrality of the father-husband for the family, and the manner in which his action involved the total group. Specifically, the new-born child was indissolubly bound up with the father (a fact which is central to the hope of David following the death of his child, cf. 2 Sam. 12:22ff). The father's action automatically involved the total family, apart from individual volitional decision. Thus, the new-born infant was a member of the covenant community through his father's identification with that community.

Consequently there was never in the Old Testament a time of personal decision when the youth identified himself as a practicing member of the community of faith. Through corporate solidarity with his father he had been part of that community from the moment of birth. It was for this reason that a male child could be circumcised so early as the eighth day, his circumcision signifying identification with the worshipping community of faith, or the "church" to use the New Testament terminology.

Guilt and Individual Responsibility

What was the Old Testament understanding concerning moral accountability, inherited guilt, and individual responsibility? Each of these is of extreme significance for understanding the relationship of the child to the church, and, more significantly, his relationship to God. If there are clear cut biblical emphases concerning these principles, then primary foundations for a theology of children and the church may have been established.

First, with regard to moral accountability, the Old Testament presupposes that men are morally accountable to God, but it offers little help concerning a specific age before which one might be treated as "innocent" and after which one is morally responsible.

In all probability Israelite society recognized that children at some juncture reached a rational, decision-making point beyond which they became responsible for their own actions. It is quite significant that this age was never specified. The Old Testament assumes no change in the relationship of the child to the worshipping community before and after such a time of individual responsibility.

The age of about twelve did emerge within Judaism as the age at which a young man assumed full responsibilities within the worshipping community, but it is hazardous to read such practices into the Old Testament apart from any biblical evidence.

Thus, there is no evidence within the Old Testament for what is referred to among some churches as the "age of accountability" as it relates to the relationship of the child and the worshipping community, or to the child and God on the more personal level.

Second, more significant for Israel than the relatively modern view of "age of accountability," was the principle of inherited guilt. There are sufficient references within the biblical material to suggest that the sins of the fathers were thought of as visited upon the children.

Fundamental to the idea of inherited guilt was the view of corporate personality within Israel. Just as a child was bound up in the covenant because of his absorption into the father's action, so was the child enmeshed in the guilt of the father. Few passages within the Old Testament are clearer than the second commandment, "For I the Lord your God am a jealous God, visiting the iniquity of the fathers upon the children to the third and the fourth generation of those who hate me, but showing steadfast love to thousands of those who love me and keep my commandments" (Ex. 20:5).

God, likewise, "will by no means clear the guilty, visiting the iniquity of the fathers upon the children and the children's children, to the third and the fourth generation" (Ex. 34:7; cf. also, Lev. 20:5; 26:39-42; Num. 14:18, 33; 1 Kings 21:29; Job 21:19; Psalm 37:28; Isa. 14:20, 21; 65:6, 7; Jer. 32:18; Dan. 6:24).

Examination of the thirteen contexts cited above reveals that in no instance was the child morally responsible for the action of his father. The passages speak only of the way in which a man's descendants bear the consequences of the father's sin. Also of importance is the fact that the condition produced by bearing the iniquity of the fathers is normally some type of calamity; exile (Lev. 26:39-43), national destruction or calamity (1 Kings 21:29 ; Isa. 14:20, 21, Babylon), or an undefined assertion of reprisal (cf. Ex. 20:5 et al.). Only in one extreme case, involving the worship of Molech and the practice of child sacrifice, was expulsion from the covenant community viewed as a possibility (Lev. 20:1-5).

Thus, it is legitimate to infer that the visitation of the father's sin upon the children did not involve separation from God as expressed through the worshipping community. The biblical writer meant to infer that children bore the ill effects of their heritage, not that they were themselves morally responsible, to use a modern term, and thus subject to expulsion from divine fellowship and the worshipping community.

The Old Testament had no view of inherited guilt within those passages which refer to the sins of the fathers as visited upon their children, and their children's children. Not even in Psalm 51:5 is the writer describing inherited guilt. (Some do feel that the verse rests behind Paul's statement in Ephesians 2:3.) In all probability the writer of Psalm 51 sought to express man's total incorporation into a humanity which was sinful and iniquitous. Viewing his own life, he saw himself as sinful from the moment of conception, to say nothing of birth.

Considering the paucity of evidence elsewhere in the Old Testament, it is hazardous to build a doctrine of "original sin" on a single verse. That the psalmist expressed the biblical view that all men are involved with humanity in sin, that every man has a propensity to sin, is justifiable on the basis of numerous contexts. But it is tenuous in the extreme to suggest that he sought to formulate a statement on biologically transmitted "original sin."

It remains to be said, however, that even if one should legitimately conclude that the Old Testament spoke of inherited guilt such a view did not exclude the individual from the community of faith. Although the child might have been viewed as in someway sharing in sinful humanity, this did not exclude him from fellowship with God. His guilt was reconciled within the context of both divine fellowship and the worshipping community, and did not effect a breach of that fellowship.

Third, the problem of the relationship between the sin of one generation and the judgment of another became so pronounced in Israel that two prophets in later Israel dealt pointedly with the issue (cf. Deut. 24:16; 2 Kings 14:6). By the time of Jeremiah, the principle of a generation reaping the judgment of their parent's sin had led to the extreme view that the generation of Jeremiah and Ezekiel was not morally responsible for its own situation. It was simply bearing the iniquity of its fathers.

This tendency to absolve one's self of personal responsibility by appealing to the ancient principle that the guilt of the fathers was visited upon succeeding generations led to the double prophetic emphasis that (1) men are individually responsible for their own sin, and (2) they are not morally responsible for the sins of their parents.

By the time of Jeremiah there had emerged the popular proverb, "The fathers have eaten sour grapes, and the children's teeth are set on edge" (Jer. 31:29). Or, the fathers sin but the children bear the judgment. Jeremiah said the time would come when "every one shall die for his own sin; each man who eats sour grapes, his teeth shall be set on edge" (Jer. 29:30). It is highly significant that Jeremiah's teaching of the new covenant follows (Jer. 31:31ff). The new covenant is still made with "the house of Israel and the house of Judah" (v. 31), but its individualistic nature is such as to underscore that God will deal with a man on the basis of his own relationship with God and the covenant written "upon their hearts" (v. 33).

Ezekiel built upon Jeremiah's emphasis on individual responsibility, and by the use of a classic illustration made it clear that a man would not bear the guilt of his father (Ezek. 18:1ff). Predicated on the assumption that "the soul that sins shall die" (18:4), Ezekiel used three generations to illustrate his point. (1) He first described a man who was righteous—he would live because he was righteous (18:5-9). (2) Ezekiel then described the man's son as a robber, a shedder of blood; as one who was the antithesis of a righteous man. This man would not live because he had a righteous father, but rather ". . . shall surely die; his blood shall be upon himself" (Ezek. 18:10-13).

(3) Then Ezekiel described a third generation, the grandson of the righteous man and the son of the unrighteous. This man who "sees all the sins which his father has done, and fears . . . he shall not die for his father's iniquity; he shall surely live" (vs. 14-17). Thus, in what is perhaps the most pointed argument against inherited guilt in biblical literature, Ezekiel clearly indicated that each person is judged on the basis of his own relationship to God; not upon the basis of guilt inherited from his parents.

Fourth, in summary, two conclusions should be reiterated. (1) The Old Testament did not deal with a counterpart to the modern phrase "age of accountability." Nor does the Old Testament lend evidence to the view of inherited guilt. Rather, it insists that in view of individual responsibility each man is ultimately judged on the basis of his own righteousness or unrighteousness.

(2) Even if one should legitimately conclude that the Old Testament taught a specific age of moral accountability and inherited guilt, one would still be hard pressed to illustrate on the basis of Old Testament evidence that either inherited guilt or reaching the "age of accountability" constituted a breach between the child and the worshipping community.

The Old Testament deals forthrightly with man's sinful nature. This is beyond question. But one's sin is dealt with within the broader context of divine fellowship and the worshipping community. A male child was initiated into the worshipping community through the act of circumcision, and he was never viewed as outside the bounds of that fellowship in the sense of entering into some kind of noncovenantal quality of life within Israel.

In such an extreme case, however, those involved were probably driven completely outside the Israelite community, not simply outside the worshipping community, as though one could remain an Israelite, but not part of the worshipping community. Such a dichotomy is foreign to Old Testament covenant precepts altogether. There was no qualitative distinction between the Israelite community at large and the so-called worshipping community.

Family Structure within the Old Testament

One of the barriers between contemporary attitudes concerning the child and the church on the one hand, and ancient Israel on the other is the nature of family structure in Israel. The father acted for the entire family, and the family was in turn responsible for individual members to a degree that is not often experienced in contemporary society. There are two characteristics of Israelite family structure which are especially pertinent to a study of the child and the faith community.

1. The primacy of the father-husband within the Israelite family.— Within Israelite families, from every conceivable perspective the father was "head of the house" in the most literal sense. Infant boys were initiated into the covenant community by virture of the infants' identification with the larger faith community through their fathers' participation in the faith community. The male child was in the covenant community because of his father.

The female was set within a totally different context within Old Testament culture than in modern Western culture. The numerous ways in which the female was subordinate to the father-husband is indicative of the manner in which the male dominated society. The most obvious indication of their subordinate role, even in religious areas, is the fact that circumcision as a sign of the covenant automatically restricted direct covenant membership to male members of the community.

Female members of society were within the covenant, to be sure, but they were so because of their relationship to a male. For all of her life woman remained a minor in Old Testament thought. The wife could not inherit from her husband, nor could daughters inherit from their father, except when there was no male heir (Num. 27:8). The Decalogue enumerates a man's possessions and includes his wife among them (Ex. 20:17; Deut. 5:21). A girl or married woman could make a vow to God, but it had to be ratified by her husband or father, and if that ratification was withheld the vow was null and void (Num. 30:4-17). For all of this, however, those rare passages which portray the intimacy of family life show that an Israelite wife was loved and listened to by her husband. (Cf. 1 Sam. 1:4-8, 22-23; 2 Kings 4:8-24; Prov. 31:10-31; and Roland de Vaux, *Ancient Israel: Its Life and Institutions.*)

All of this underscores the manner in which the father-husband acted on behalf of the total family. The priority of the father-husband for the Israelite family is clear in three ways: (1) in the entrance of the infant male child into the covenant of faith, (2) in the means which the father-husband identified female members of society with the covenant community, (3) in the action of the father on behalf of the family group as manifested in his ratifying the religious vow(s) of daughters or wife. Even in religious matters, he was the key to the entrance of the family group into the community of faith.

One should not conclude that this father-dominated family structure mitigated against the best interest of the family. It should be quickly pointed out that the father and the home assumed primary significance for the well-being of the family in all areas of life. Especially was the home the center of education and religious training. The aims of education were twofold: (1) the transmission of God's covenant with his people and the history of the outworkings of that covenant, and (2) instruction in the ethical conduct of life. In this regard, it was incumbent primarily upon every father of a family to impart instruction to his children, at least during their early childhood. The early memories of the Exodus and the fear of the Lord are to be retold in the presence of children (Ex. 10:2; 12:26-27). Abraham is to instruct not only his children but his entire household in the way of the Lord (Gen. 18:19).

The father also gave his son a professional education, and trades were normally hereditary. One of the Rabbis suggested that "He who does not teach his son a useful trade is bringing him up to be a thief." It was probably because of the teaching role of the father that priests were also later called father (cf. Judg. 17:10; 18:19).

2. The family as the focus of religious instruction.—The center of religious instruction for the child was the home, not the shrine or temple. In older Israel the father served as priest, offering sacrifice for the family (cf. Gen. 8:20ff; Gen. 12:7ff; *et al.*). Even circumcision was carried out in earlier times by the father (Gen. 21:4). Later circumcision was performed by a professional specialist (cf. 1 Macc. 1:61), but it was never carried out in the sanctuary or by a priest. It was essentially a home-centered ceremony.

There are two primary emphases upon the home as the focus of religious instruction which are significant for this essay. First, the Shema (Deut. 6:4-9), the most important set of teachings after the Decalogue, is to be imparted within the family circle:

"Hear, O Israel: The Lord our God is one Lord and you shall love the Lord your God with all your heart, and with all your soul, and with all your might. And these words which I command you this day shall be upon your heart; and you shall teach them to your children, and shall talk of them when you sit in your house, and when you walk by the way" (Deut. 6:4-9).

The use of the word "Lord" (Yahweh or Jehovah) is significant, for it is never used except to show covenant relationship with Yahweh, the God of Israel. Yet, those within the family circle, including the children, are to be taught this central declaration of the covenant of faith. This example does not prove that children were members of the covenant community in the same sense that children "join" a church. However, the absence of evidence concerning a time of public identification with the worshipping community, analogous to "joining the church," can only lead one to conclude that the children were within the covenant community. Apparently the instruction was designed to strengthen them in their covenant faith.

Second, originally the Passover was a family-centered observance (cf. Ex. 12:1ff; 14ff; 21ff) and had instructive value for the children: "And when your children say to you, 'What do you mean by this service?' you shall say, 'It is the sacrifice of the Lord's passover, for he passed over the houses of the people of Israel in Egypt, when he slew the Egyptians but spared our houses' " (Ex. 12:26f).

Both the Shema and the Passover, therefore, illustrate how faith was cultivated apart from formal religious structures.

Contrary to common attitudes, there was not in ancient Israel a shrine on every plot of ground, analogous to the "church on every corner" in our own country. There were numerous local shrines, to be sure. But in all probability many families doubtless worshipped most frequently in the home, and quite seldom appeared at the Temple in Jerusalem, and only slightly more often at localized sites such as Shiloh or Bethel. Neither did the religious calendar demand the presence of worshippers so frequently as do the calendars of most contemporary churches.

The fact that religious experience existed within the framework of the home, parallel with the organized structure of religion at the holy sites, is evidence for the fact that there was no necessity for a child to make a public commitment at such a shrine. The child grew up in the faith as he shared in the nurture of a godly family. *The only "church" he immediately knew was the family circle, the only "priest" his own father.*

Thus, the distinction between the structure of an Israelite family and a contemporary family in Western society is a clear reason why many today experience problems with regard to the child and the church that would have never emerged in ancient Israel. The priority of the father in ancient Israel leads to the inclusion of family members within the covenant on the basis of the father's covenant relationship. For many in Israel the family-centered nature of religion meant that the child not only was born into the faith but that the primary nurture he received was from the family circle, not the institution of shrine and temple. Also, religion was largely home-centered in its personal development and nurture.

Implications for a Contemporary Reappraisal

Having surveyed the child in the context of the Old Testament covenant community, what conclusions emerge which may be helpful in seeking to formulate a theology of children and the church?

First, the child entered the covenant community through corporate solidarity with his father. The principle of corporate personality is fundamental to an understanding of how Israel conceived an infant to be part of the faith community, apart from personal commitment.

Second, the family constituted the context of religious instruction and, in many instances, of worship as well. Contrary to the picture of the institutional aspects of religion which triumphed in the literature of Israel, home worship was probably much more significant than is normally stressed. Thus, Old Testament thought patterns would never have faced the problem many confront in modern society with regard to the issue of "joining the church."

Children were members of the covenant community through identification with the male parent. Circumcision was practiced in the home, religious instruction was within the home, and the home was also a primary agent of worship for the family circle. In all probability pilgrimages to Jerusalem were exceptional events, and even visits to the secondary sanctuaries were most likely less frequent than was worship in the home.

Third, there is no apparent narrative within the Old Testament which deals with the personal commitment of a native Israelite to the covenant community. Only outsiders, later referred to as proselytes, faced the decision of whether or not to identify with God's people.

Although each succeeding generation reaffirmed its commitment in general terms, there was no "once-for-all" time when an individual assumed covenant obligations. The only option for a native Israelite was the rejection of faith, not its acceptance; and even this rejection was not allowed according to the terms of the covenant, but was a dishonorable act.

Fourth, the principle of covenant theology sets the child within the community of faith from the time of birth.

Although I am by no means suggesting this as a Christian pattern or theology, the application of Old Testament covenant theology to the Christian church would imply the following. (1) A child born of Christian parents and nurtured in the training of a Christian home is included within the Christian community of faith. (2) His personal decision concerns whether or not he will repudiate the faith into which he was born and reared, not whether he will "accept" that faith; and repudiation would be dishonorable. (3) His worship would center in the home and climax in the church.

(4) His home would recapture its central role in religious experience. His parents would recognize a direct responsibility for his total welfare, and would fulfil that responsibility by seeking to provide the necessary context conducive to educational motivation, ethically responsible character, and a profession or trade commensurate with his abilities. (5) The church would have so permeated his world that there would be no wall of separation between the remainder of his life and the church. "Joining the church" would lose much of its definitive nature and become simply the natural outgrowth of his own Christian heritage and outlook.

(6) The child would never face the possible frustration of knowing the nurture of a Christian home and the loving guidance of church leaders, only to find that once he reached an accepted chronological age he was treated as standing outside the covenant faith by home, church, and God. He would never feel he must now do something to recapture the quality of love and joy that he had earlier known of God, home, and church within the covenant community. In essence, the Old Testament view of covenant theology would take seriously the presupposition that a child who is once within the saving grace of God is never abandoned.

Obviously, I am not proposing this as a final statement on the theology of the child and the church. But I am proposing that these conclusions are soundly based upon the Old Testament, and that they should be considered seriously in seeking to understand the relationship of the child to the church. One may decide that the Old Testament should be dismissed as irrelevant, that nothing revealed concerning the child and the community of faith has any binding power on those now seeking to formulate a theology of the child and the church. But to do this is radically to sever the Old Testament revelation from Christian scripture, a practice declared heretical for almost two thousand years.

Despite the strange sound of its notes, the Old Testament echo of covenant theology should be heard concerning the child and the church. Covenant theology could offer positive guidance as many today seek an answer to the questions concerning the relationship of the child and the church. Modifications of the Old Testament view of covenant theology appears to offer greatest hope for the reconciliation of problems faced by those who deal seriously with a theology of children and the church.

3

New Testament Passages About Children
William B. Coble

One of the most firmly established facts of Baptist history is that we have sought to be in theory and practice a people of *the Book*. Although the Old Testament must hold a vital place, the New Testament has been and is the center of our being. We hold that when it is interpreted under the guidance of the Holy Spirit, the New Testament is man's adequate guide in matters of spiritual understanding and living.

When a question arises concerning spiritual truth or the propriety of some practice, one of the first steps we normally take is to study the New Testament teachings on the subject. Such a study is usually begun with a feeling of quiet confidence that in his Word God has provided the guidance which we need. Prayerful, diligent Bible study, we believe, will open the way to the solution of the problem being faced. This fact has made a vital contribution to stability, spiritual power, and effectiveness of labor in Baptist life. No person who holds dear the form and spirit of Baptist work would want to suggest any other approach. That is certainly not the purpose of this writing.

Yet on the subject of the relation of children to God and to the church our attitude toward the New Testament may have served us as a two-edged sword. One edge is encountered at the beginning of a study and is formed by the blending of that spirit of confidence with two other feelings: (1) our children are one of the greatest values of our life—therefore the New Testament will surely provide adequate guidance for meeting their every spiritual need; (2) the task of providing spiritual nurture for our children is terribly complex. It involves almost every idea and question which is a part of the spiritual experience and discipline of adults *plus* a multitude of other psychological and educational problems. Therefore we need all the spiritual guidance we can find, and what source of help can be compared with the New Testament?

The other edge of the sword may be encountered shortly after the study is begun, and it may be less obvious than the first one. The fact that the New Testament says so little about children and the church's treatment of them can easily lull us into the false assumption that children are to be treated in the same manner as adults. Children's spiritual needs are not the same as those of adults; so they cannot be met through the same practices and procedures which meet adults' needs.

If one does begin studying the New Testament with a calm expectation of finding clear and adequate teachings on this subject, he will experience a sudden shock. Two facts stand out quickly: (1) the New Testament says very little about children in the sense with which we are using the word, although its vocabulary gives a prominent place to family terms used in a spiritual sense, such as father, son, and child; (2) what the New Testament does say gives us very limited instruction about the what, how, or why of proper Christian methods of meeting children's spiritual needs.

All of our sentimental expressions of Jesus' love for little children notwithstanding, the New Testament is a book written about, to, and for adults. Several things probably contributed to this situation, of which two are most significant:

(1) The nature of the Christian message and movement.—In the beginning the gospel was necessarily addressed to the adults of an almost totally pagan world. It sought to call them out of that world to find in Christ the fulfilment of their own personal and spiritual needs.

(2) The powerful expectation of Christ's return to the earth in a short time (cf. 1 Thess. 4:13-18, etc.).—When we consider the New Testament's emphasis on this subject, it seems quite possible that the apostolic leaders saw no reason to try to establish a system of nurture and instruction to be used on generations of children whom they did not expect to be born. That several generations of early Christians

took this hope seriously is indicated by the long delay in the development of any recognized method of training the children of Christian parents.

This situation's significance becomes more clear as we consider the fact that nearly all of the early disciples were of the Jewish, Greek, or Roman culture groups. All of these societies had high ideals concerning the training of children, especially the boys, and concerning the methods by which they should be prepared to perpetuate the traditions of their heritage. Yet it is clear that the early churches provided special instruction only for those who were preparing to become active believers, who were called "catechumens," a matter which is developed more fully in chapter 5 of this book.

Although New Testament teachings on the subject of the child and his relation to Christ and the church are limited in number and content, what we do find must be studied carefully. In fact, we need studies in much greater detail than the limits of this chapter will allow. By making such a study, we will be enabled to clarify a perspective. We must both face the problems which exist in our life and survey correctly the guidance which the Scriptures give us. The New Testament's teachings must be the foundation on which we stand as we seek ways to be followed and methods to be used in achieving a more complete approach to the matter.

The Gospels

The Gospels are the logical place to begin the study of almost any New Testament subject. It is particularly important to see if Jesus had anything to say on the matter. In the Gospels we find that many words are used with varying meanings. The Greek word which is translated "son" is used in the four Gospels over 220 times. Two related words which are usually translated as "child (children)" are used more than 50 times. Yet there are only five statements from Jesus' lips which make reference to children in our sense of the term. Parallel forms of three of the five statements are found in Matthew, Mark, and Luke; and Matthew and Luke contain parallel forms of the other two. John's Gospel contains no direct reference to our subject. In studying Jesus' words it is often as important to establish what they do *not* say as it is to see what they do say.

Minor References.—Two references deal with our subject in such an oblique and general way that they are mentioned only for completeness' sake. The first is a statement on parent-child relationships, "If ye then, being evil, know how to give good gifts unto your children, how much more shall your Father which is in heaven give good things to them that ask him?" (Matt. 7:11). In the parallel statement in Luke 11:13 we find "the Holy Spirit" instead of "good gifts," evidently the meaning being that the Holy Spirit is the choicest gift which God can bestow on man.

Here Jesus acknowledged a fact of life—parents' concern for their children and ability to care for them. He used that fact as the background for teaching the readiness and ability of God to provide for his children. This thought is similar to something which Paul said, "Children ought not to lay up for the parents, but the parents for the children" (2 Cor. 12:14). The words of both Jesus and Paul are simple observations of normal patterns of human conduct, and neither expression has any direct bearing on our theme of study.

The second statement of this group presents the potentially divisive nature of the gospel. "The brother shall deliver up the brother to death, and the father the child: and the children shall rise up against their parents, and cause them to be put to death. . . . For I am come to set a man at variance against his father, and the daughter against her mother, and the daughter in law against her mother in law. . . . a man's foes shall be they of his own household. He that loveth father or mother more than me is not worthy of me: and he that loveth son or daughter more than me is not worthy of me" (Matt. 10:21-37). "If any man come to me, and hate not his father, and mother, and wife, and children, and brethren, and sisters, yea, and his own life also, he cannot be my disciple" (Luke 14:26).

In these statements Jesus pointed out the fact that discipleship often forces a person to choose his values and his companions, emphasizing the fact that individual loyalty to Christ may cause the rupture of major earthly loyalties. This is the only way in which these passages have any direct bearing upon our subject, because Jesus was treating the principle of parent-offspring relationships rather than adult relationships with minor children.

Major Passages.—The remaining three passages found in Jesus' teachings do enter directly into our considerations. In dealing with them, however, it is vital that we be faithful to the Scriptures. This means that our interpretation must be in harmony with the intended purpose of the speaker, Jesus, and of the Gospel writers. Too long people have engaged in the practice of claiming biblical authority for ideas and practices of their own choosing. This they do by taking biblical words out of their context and giving them meanings which were never intended by the speaker or writer.

An illustration of this practice is provided by the famous case of the mountaineer pastor, who may have been fictitious. For a sermon against the then-new hair style, the topknot, he took his text *from* Matthew 24:17, "Let him which is on the housetop not come down to take any thing out of his house." His subject: "Top Not, Come Down." His text contained words taken directly from the Bible; but he was totally untrue to the Bible, as he put his own meaning into Matthew's words.

We are obligated to avoid such distortions of the Scriptures. To do so we must try to determine what the passages say *and* what they do not say, considering fully the setting of the passage and the author's purpose, as well as the words which he chose to use. Only by being faithful to the meaning which the writer sought to convey can we find in the Scriptures true directions for our thought and practice with regard to children in relation to the church.

Jesus' Blessing of the Children (Mark 10:13-16; Matt. 19:13-15; Luke 18:15-17).—Mark's account of this incident is the fullest: "They brought young children to him, that he should touch them: and his disciples rebuked those that brought them. But when Jesus saw *it,* he was much displeased, and said unto them, Suffer the little children to come unto me, and forbid them not: for of such is the kingdom of God. Verily I say unto you, whosoever shall not receive the kingdom of God as a little child, he shall not enter therein. And he took them up in his arms, put his hands upon them, and blessed them" (10:13-16).

It is difficult to comprehend the degree to which usually competent interpreters drift off into sentimental ramblings when they begin a consideration of this passage. The general practice seems to be to forget the text completely and engage in emotional spiritualizing. The picture which the text presents is that of people bringing their children to Jesus with the request that he bestow a Jewish blessing upon them, which included laying his hands upon them in a recognized ceremonial form. The practice was ancient, the most significant Old Testament accounts of it being the blessings pronounced by Isaac on Jacob and Esau (Gen. 27) and the blessings which Jacob bestowed on his twelve sons from his deathbed (Gen. 49).

The foundation of the action was the belief that one's relationship to God could be used to bring benefit to the life of another—or injury in the pronouncement of a curse, as in the experience of Balaam (Num. 22:6). This was not the mere mouthing of words or the voicing of pious hopes for "good luck." It was the expression of real power to shape the destiny of a life. That was the reason that Isaac could not retract the blessing which he had pronounced upon Jacob and give it to Esau (Gen. 27). Once pronounced, the blessing was unchangeable and was a power operative in the life of the person on whom it had been bestowed. Too, the nearer the person who pronounced it was to God, the more certain would be his ability to bring good into the life of the person whom he blessed. So it is no wonder that parents felt that for Jesus to lay his hands on their children would guarantee for them a bountiful future.

Mark had been careful to show what wonderful things had been made to happen by Jesus' hands. Simon Peter's mother-in-law (1:31) and a leper (1:41) were healed. Jairus' daughter (5:41) was raised from the dead. A crowd of over five thousand was fed from five pieces of bread and two fish (6:35-44). The thinking of the people was summarized in the question, "From whence hath this *man* these things? and what wisdom is this which is given unto him, that even such mighty works are wrought by his hands?" (6:2). Would anything be more natural than for people to want Jesus' hands to touch their children in blessing?

Neither is it any wonder that the disciples would try to "protect" Jesus from adults who were bringing their children. Outside of the home, the ancient world held a very low estimate of children. Usually the child was not even to be seen among adults, certainly not to be heard. An important Jewish leader was not expected to waste his time with children.

One prominent rabbi, Dosa B. Archinos, said, "Morning sleep, midday wine, the chatter of children, and staying in resorts where common people meet bring a man out of the world." So the society of Jesus' day would think that the disciples were quite normal in feeling that the demands which blessing the children would make on Jesus' time and attention were totally out of place. This is just one in a series of incidents which Mark used to show that the disciples did not understand Jesus' mission (note particularly 1:36-38; 6:36; 8:14-21,32-33; 9:5,32,38; 10:35-45). As far as the disciples were concerned, children had nothing to contribute to the establishing of the kind of kingdom which they had in mind.

Jesus' response to the disciples is an aspect of the constant theme of the Synoptic Gospels—Matthew, Mark, and Luke. Jesus' ministry was for the benefit of the helpless, the needy, the outcast. He had come to give himself to and for those who had nothing of their own to give. No group more completely embodied the quality of helplessness than did the children. So he took them in his arms, laid his hands on them, and blessed them. That is, within the area of the seekers' request he gave himself completely to them. By taking the children into his arms he went beyond the request to lay his hands on them.

In interpreting the passage two things must be remembered. First, in *no* sense are we to think of these children as being or as becoming followers of Jesus. They were brought to Jesus solely for the purpose of receiving a Jewish blessing. Matthew shows that Jesus, after giving the blessing, went on his way. So there is *no* sense in which this passage can be taken as a basis for the type of evangelism in which small children are asked to make a commitment of their life to Jesus Christ as Lord and Saviour. True, the spiritual power of his life had been brought to bear upon the children whom he had blessed. But there is no way that we can be true to the text and say that they responded to him in the kind of faith which brings the salvation which the New Testament offers to men in the resurrected Lord.

The second thing to be remembered is that the primary purpose of this story is found in the way in which Jesus used the situation as the basis for teaching *adults*. The main point of the passage is found in the words, "for of such is the kingdom of God" (Mark 10:14). "Of such" is the translation of a possessive form which means that the kingdom *belongs to* a certain kind of people; it does not mean that the kingdom is *made up* of a certain kind of people. Therefore determining the meaning of "of such" is the central problem in understanding these verses. The expression clearly cannot mean that these particular children, the ones who had been blessed, were in the kingdom of God. "Of such" describes a quality; it does not show identity. Still it does not mean that children like them possess the kingdom.

Two lines of thought have been followed in interpreting what Jesus meant by the term. The most commonly accepted way understands the words to suggest inner characteristics of childlikeness, such as humility, meekness, trust, obedience, or joy. The list of the virtues of childhood which interpreters have suggested is almost endless, and most of these virtues are far more imagined than real.

This interpretation has two major weaknesses: (1) It leaves the description of the nature of the one who possesses the kingdom to the imagination of the individual, since the understanding of the inner characteristics of childlikeness which Jesus may have meant varies greatly with people. (2) Setting up this quality of personality as a prerequisite to entry into the kingdom finally makes it a form of work or way of proving merit. This is because the person who does not possess these qualities must somehow effect them within himself in order to be accepted into the kingdom.

The other view of "of such" is that it refers to the actual outward situation, a condition of weakness, helplessness, or even worthlessness in the eyes of those around them. The children whom Jesus had blessed possessed neither the power to take anything nor the right to claim anything for themselves. It is to this kind of person that the kingdom of God is given. That God has willed to act in this way is one of the major themes of the New Testament.

Jesus said: "Fear not, little flock; for it is your Father's good pleasure to give you the kingdom" (Luke 12:32). One of the most important statements concerning the nature of Christ in the New Testament begins with Jesus' words, "I thank thee, O Father, Lord of heaven and earth, that thou hast hid these things from the wise and prudent, and hast revealed them unto babes: even so, Father; for so it seemed good in thy sight" (Luke 10:21; parallel in Matt. 11:25-26). Paul reminded the Corinthians that "God hath chosen the foolish things of the world to confound the wise; and God hath chosen the weak things of the world to confound the things which are mighty" (1 Cor. 1:27).

This kind of childlikeness is not one which can be imitated nor be effected by one's own effort; it can only be recognized as the true state of the human being before God. This was what Jesus meant when he said, "Whosoever shall not receive the kingdom of God as a little child, he shall not enter therein" (Mark 10:15).

So we must conclude that the Gospel writers' purpose in recording this incident was to use the little child as an object lesson. Through this adults can more clearly understand the nature of God's kingdom and the way they may enter it. This is quite different from the tendency to interpret the passage in such a loose way that it is used as the basis for the idea that children are to be brought into the kingdom of God because they who enter it must be childlike. This is saying to children, "If you believe in the way that an adult believes, you may enter the kingdom."

The Lesson on True Greatness (Matt. 18:1-5; Mark 9:33-37; Luke 9:46-48).—Matthew's statement of this incident is probably the clearest: "At the same time came the disciples unto Jesus, saying, Who is the greatest in the kingdom of heaven? And Jesus called a little child unto him, and set him in the midst of them, and said, Verily I say unto you, Except ye be converted, and become as little children, ye shall not enter into the kingdom of heaven.

"Whosoever therefore shall humble himself as this little child, the same is greatest in the kingdom of heaven. And whoso shall receive one such little child in my name receiveth me" (18:1-5).

The age-old problem of man, the desire for the recognition of rank, has always been a source of special problem in the Orient. The frequence of its appearance in the Gospels points to the seriousness of the problem, not only among the early apostles, but also throughout the early history of the church. Every movement of men has had some type of standard for determining the means by which individuals might attain to recognized greatness within the group.

The disciples wanted Jesus to give a clear statement which would define those standards in his kingdom. That would make it possible for each person to establish his own goals in terms of what he was willing to do. Some people are willing to run greater risks and expend greater efforts than are others, provided the incentive justifies the danger and the labor. The true nature of any movement can be seen only in its best example. This is because the heartbeat of any organized effort is found in the methods by which a person attains preeminence within the group. So every disciple must understand that the uniqueness of Jesus' kingdom includes a standard of recognized greatness which is the opposite of the standards found in most human movements.

Jesus' statement shows the necessity of a transformation of concepts as well as the need of excellence of conduct. He used two methods of expressing the thought. The first was a word picture. "Be converted" is the translation of a word which means "be turned around," or "turn yourself around." If the disciple maintains the viewpoint which characterizes human movements, he cannot see Jesus' ideal. To understand Jesus' concept of the ideal citizen of the kingdom, one must choose to turn his back upon the standards which ordinarily motivate men.

Jesus' second method of establishing his thought was the use of an object lesson, the person of a small child. His meaning must be understood in the sense which was found in his description of the way by which a person might enter the kingdom. The great one in his kingdom is the one who recognizes his own helplessness and dependence, even his worthlessness. This is the only kind of person for whom the life of trustful obedience to God is possible. Anyone who entertains an idea of self's worth, position, or power will be sorely tempted to assume the position of God's instructor.

Simon Peter took this upon himself when he began to reprimand Jesus for telling the disciples that being the Christ meant that he must be rejected by the religious leaders, suffer, die, and be raised again (Mark 8:32). The little child lives with the consciousness of utter personal helplessness and total dependence upon someone else. To the child the greatness which comes by way of status is meaningless. So the disciple has no reason to be a status seeker, nor to be impressed with a person who attains status among men.

When Jesus added, "Whoso shall receive one such little child in my name receiveth me" (Matt. 18:5), he was describing the person who has attained that standard. Jesus meant that one gives to a child the respectful, kind, considerate, thoughtful reception with which he would honor the King himself. But even more significant than that is the realization that our King's *first* command is to meet the needs of such a lowly and weak person, one who has nothing to give to anyone. In Christ's kingdom one does not show supreme loyalty by saying to him, "Your wish is my command." That loyalty to Christ is shown when one meets one of the helpless and needy little children and acts out the motto, "*Your* need is my Lord's command to me." This is one of three places in which Matthew describes Jesus as identifying himself openly with the lowly and needy (see also 10:42 and 25:31-46).

So in this statement, just as in the passage which describes his blessing of the children, Jesus made use of the child to teach adults.

Neither passage gives us any concrete guidance with regard to the question of how to meet the spiritual needs of children.

The Value of a Little One's Life (Mark 9:42; Luke 17:1-2; Matt. 18:6-14).—The last statement of Jesus which seems to pertain to children places emphasis upon a little one's life. There is reason to question whether or not he was talking about children in his original statement. There is far more variety in the forms of this utterance than there is in the forms of the other statements. Mark's account gives its simplest expression, making it a part of the discussion which followed Jesus' rebuke of the apostle John for having told someone to quit casting out demons in Jesus' name "because he followeth not us" (9:38).

In the larger passage, Mark 9:38-48, there seems to be a progression in Jesus' thought: (1) a person cannot perform a miracle in his name, then speak evil of him lightly (v. 39); (2) if a person is not actively opposing us, he must be on our side (v. 40); (3) full reward will be given to any person who honors one of Jesus' disciples, even with so much as a glass of water (v. 41); (4) there is great danger in bringing harm to one of his disciples (vv. 42-48).

The implication seems to be that John should have honored the one who was acting in Jesus' name instead of exposing himself to great punishment by putting a stumbling block in the way of the man's faithfulness. The section (vv. 42-48) begins with the statement, "Whosoever shall offend one of these little ones that believe in me, it is better for him that a millstone were hanged about his neck, and he were cast into the sea."

In Luke the statement appears as an isolated teaching. It has no direct connection with the thought of that which precedes it, the story of the rich man and the beggar (16:19-31), nor with that which follows, teaching on how a disciple should forgive a brother who has wronged him (17:3-10). Luke's wording is also quite different from that of Mark. It says, "Then said he unto the disciples, it is impossible but that offences will come: but woe unto him, through whom they come! It were better for him that a millstone were hanged about his neck, and he cast into the sea, than that he should offend one of these little ones" (17:1-2).

These two statements have in common three things which are of primary importance: (1) "Offend" is the translation of a Greek word which meant "to sin." But the root from which the word was derived pictured the act of tripping one up or causing one to stumble, particularly to fall into a trap in which he would be wounded or killed. So the point here is that of endangering a person's life, rather than causing him anger or discomfort, by leading him into sin. (2) The terrible judgment to which such exercise of influence would expose one is implied by showing that a better alternative would be to experience a death so horrible that one could never be buried. (3) For our consideration the most important term is "one of these little ones."

This is the literal translation of the Greek words; so the question to be decided is how the expression is to be interpreted. Does it refer to children—those who are physically little, or does it mean the spiritually small ones—Jesus' disciples, with no thought of age or size being involved? Nothing in Luke's statement gives us any guidance; it could be interpreted either way. The form of the statement in Mark lends itself far more naturally to the spiritual interpretation, since nothing in the context even suggests a connection with children.

It is only in Matthew's Gospel that there is any association between this statement and children. The expression is a little different from that which is found in either Mark or Luke. "But whoso shall offend one of these little ones which believe in me, it were better for him that a millstone were hanged about his neck, and that he were drowned in the depth of the sea" (Matt. 18:6). This verse follows immediately the statement in which Jesus ascribed greatness to those who become like little children, making the setting suggest that "these little ones" refers back to the child or children which he had been discussing. However, before deciding that this is conclusive evidence for settling the entire matter, another fact must be evaluated.

One of the characteristics of Matthew's Gospel is unique groupings of the teachings of Jesus. Five major sections of Matthew are composed of collections of Jesus' teachings, most of which seem to be scattered almost at random throughout Mark and Luke. Each of these collections is composed of teachings which are similar in emphasis. Since this is true, there seems to be little reason to doubt that Matthew intended to suggest that "these little ones" be interpreted as children. So one can take the clause "these little ones which believe in me" (v. 6), which in the Greek text is exactly the same wording as is found in Mark 9:42, and build a case for the evangelizing of young children. In doing so one should realize that the weight of the evidence in the rest of the New Testament is against this application.

Matthew 18:7-14 gives a more extensive treatment of the tragedy of causing offense than is found in either Luke 17:1 or Mark 9:43-48. The passage begins by stating the paradox of the unavoidability of offense and the tragedy to the person who is responsible for offending (v. 7); then it describes the loss one may experience by harboring something which causes his own fall (vv. 8-9). He then speaks again of "these little ones." "Take heed that ye despise not one of these little ones; for I say unto you, That in heaven their angels do always behold the face of my Father which is in heaven" (v. 10). The idea that each little one has a personal guardian angel who has immediate access to God provides a clear statement of the value of each person.

Therefore it is not strange that at this point Matthew recorded the parable of the lost sheep (vv. 12-13). Then he concluded the emphasis with the words, "Even so it is not the will of your Father which is in heaven, that one of these little ones should perish" (v. 14). The reason for the awesome peril of causing one of the little ones to fall is that it places the responsible party in direct conflict with the will of God. The concern of God for their welfare is the supreme evidence of the true value of the little ones, whether they be the children of men or the children of the Spirit.

The only sure light which this passage sheds upon the problem which we are treating is to remind us of one of the facts which initiated the entire study of this book: the welfare of every person, small or great, is a matter of vital importance. In fact, every reference to children in the Gospels adds much to our understanding of the gospel message, but no reference gives us any significant insight into the manner in which the church should deal with children.

The Book of Acts

The book of Acts contains several references to children and the family which must be considered. Some need to be treated individually and in detail. Others will be considered in relation to subjects and in connection with passages from the Epistles.

Simon Peter's words on the day of Pentecost (Acts 2:39).—"For the promise is unto you, and to your children, and to all that are afar off, *even* as many as the Lord our God shall call." One frequently finds this verse interpreted as though it applied to the Christian and his family. To see the error of this interpretation one needs only to read Acts 2:1-40 as the unit which it is. Then the verse will be seen as the climax to the invitation offered at the close of the apostle's message on the day of Pentecost.

The setting was Jerusalem; the people who composed the crowd were Jews and Jewish proselytes. Peter's message had two purposes. The negative aim was to give a rebuttal to the accusation leveled at the disciples in verse 13, "These men are full of new wine." The positive purpose was to give a proper interpretation of the Holy Spirit's manifestations in the actions of the disciples, which had attracted the crowd.

Peter began the message by showing that this experience was a fulfilment of the promise recorded by the prophet Joel, that the Lord would pour out his Spirit in a totally new manner and power (vv. 16-21). Then he showed that the experience was the natural climax of what God had done in Jesus of Nazareth, whom they, the Jews, had crucified; but whom God had raised from the tomb and made both Lord and Christ (vv. 22-36). Their question about what they should do (v. 37) was answered, "Repent, and be baptized every one of you in the name of Jesus Christ for the remission of sins, and ye shall receive the gift of the Holy Ghost" (v. 38).

In the setting in which it was spoken this was a perfectly logical and simple answer. "Repent" meant that they must reverse their mind (thinking) about Jesus of Nazareth, and being baptized in his name meant that they were to acknowledge openly that God had made him both Lord and Christ. In this way would they receive remission (forgiveness) of their sins, particularly their mistreatment of Jesus of Nazareth, "Him . . . ye have taken, and by wicked hands have crucified and slain" (v. 23). Then they, too, would become partakers of the gift of the Holy Spirit. That gift, as it had been described by the prophet Joel (vv. 17-21), was the promise to which Peter referred in verse 39.

One might list four recipients of the promise: you, your children, all that are afar off, and as many as the Lord our God shall call. To do so, however, is to miss the point of the verse, which is that the promise is for everyone whom the Lord may call. This is one of several statements in Acts designed to show God's purpose to bring salvation to all men in Jesus Christ (cf. 1:8; 10:35; 13:47; 26:19-20; 28:28).

"Those who are afar off" takes in the Gentile nations. "You and your children" represented the whole of Judaism, having the same significance here that it has in two passages connected with the passion: "His blood *be* on us, and on our children" (Matt. 27:25), and "Daughters of Jerusalem, weep not for me, but weep for yourselves, and for your children" (Luke 23:28). As he was speaking to Jews, Simon Peter told them that God's purpose in Christ was *first* for them, but that it did reach out to include all others who would come under the sovereignty of God. So the focus of the passage is upon God's dealings with the nations of the world.

To interpret Acts 2:39 as though "you and your children" meant that the gospel promises are extended to the young children of Christian people, as well as to the parents, is to yield to an appealing temptation. But to follow that interpretation is to be untrue to the record which Luke gave us. We must look elsewhere for aid as we try to determine our children's relation to the gospel and the church.

The disciples in Tyre (Acts 21:3-6).—The only other direct reference to children in the book of Acts is found in the account of Paul's last return to Jerusalem: "Now when we had discovered Cyprus, we left it on the left hand, and sailed into Syria, and landed at Tyre: for there the ship was to unlade her burden. And finding disciples, we tarried there seven days: who said to Paul through the Spirit, that he should not go up to Jerusalem. And when we had accomplished those days, we departed and went our way; and they all brought us on our way, with wives and children, till we were out of the city: and we kneeled down on the shore, and prayed. And when we had taken our leave one of another, we took ship; and they returned home again."

The only point to be made of this story is the obvious fact that the believers are clearly distinguished from their wives and children. How far we are to push this is subject to considerable discussion, particularly since neither the wives nor the children are described as believers. Only one thing can we say with certainty: this passage does not give any support to the idea that when a man became a believer, his family became "Christian" in the sense that we use the term.

The Epistles

Very few references to children are found in the Epistles, but those which we do have give us some helpful light.

Ephesians and Colossians.—The outstanding statements concerning children in the Epistles are found in parallel passages in Ephesians and Colossians. "Children, obey your parents in all things: for this is well pleasing unto the Lord. Fathers, provoke not your children to anger, lest they be discouraged" (Col. 3:20-21). "Children, obey your parents in the Lord: for this is right. Honour thy father and mother; which is the first commandment with promise; that it may be well with thee, and thou mayest live long on the earth. And, ye fathers, provoke not your children to wrath: but bring them up in the nurture and admonition of the Lord" (Eph. 6:1-4).

It is reasonable to assume that Paul was thinking in the same vein in these statements, so each passage probably throws some light upon his meaning in the other. Several things stand out in both statements:

(1) Children met with adults in the worship gatherings. Letters such as these were read aloud to the assembled group, and in each letter some words are addressed directly to the children; then the parents are addressed.

(2) Paul showed that the voluntary conduct of children is a matter of concern to God; and in a way which he did not explain, this involves children in the Christian group life. So, as children, they are not mere spectators of the religious life in which their parents were engaged; they have the responsibility of filling properly their own place in that life.

(3) The responsibility suggested here is a matter of the child's proper relationship to his home, *not* to the church. Children are to honor their parents, *not* the church leaders; and the giving of proper guidance to the child is the responsibility of the parents rather than the charge of the church or its leaders. Family life in Christ includes the provision of the instruction and the discipline of children which befits the Christian faith. These passages show that, to Paul, Christian living involved the expression of cohesiveness within the family. Each person was to fulfil his place within the group because of his relationship to the Lord and to the family.

These truths represent a vital contribution to our understanding, but there are many significant matters on which these passages give us no instruction. There is no indication of the age of those children whom Paul addressed, except the suggestion that they were still in their formative years. Whether they were to be disciplined and instructed in the Lord because they were already believers, or in order that they might become believers, is not clear. We do not know whether or not they were "church members," as we use the term. So the help which we are given with our immediate problems is relatively limited.

Pastoral Epistles.—Three brief references to children are found in 1 Timothy and Titus. In setting out the qualifications of pastoral leaders, Paul included this condition, "One that ruleth well his own house, having his children in subjection with all gravity" (1 Tim. 3:4). Then he said, "Let the deacons be the husbands of one wife, ruling their children and their own houses well" (v. 12). He told Titus, "For this cause left I thee in Crete, that thou shouldest set in order the things that are wanting, and ordain elders in every city, as I had appointed thee: If any be blameless, the husband of one wife, having faithful children not accused of riot or unruly" (1:5-6).

The point to be noted in each of these statements is that a position of spiritual leadership is to be vested in those only who are able to exercise effective control over the life of their children. The thought is expressed most clearly in Paul's parenthetical question, "(For if a man know not how to rule his own house, how shall he take care of the church of God?)" (1 Tim. 3:5).

1 Corinthians.—In 1 Corinthians Paul dealt with many problems of family relationships. Yet there is only one reference to children. "But to the rest speak I, not the Lord: If any brother hath a wife that believeth not, and she be pleased to dwell with him, let him not put her away. And the woman which hath an husband that believeth not, and if he be pleased to dwell with her, let her not leave him. For the unbelieving husband is sanctified by the wife, and the unbelieving wife is sanctified by the husband: else were your children unclean; but now are they holy. But if the unbelieving depart, let him depart. A brother or a sister is not under bondage in such cases: but God hath called us to peace" (7:12-15).

In this passage the reference to children is almost an off-handed allusion to a matter which is secondary to the main line of thought. The main point is that if a person becomes a Christian after having married and his mate is still an unbeliever who is willing to maintain the marriage, the Christian should not feel that the difference in faith demands the breaking up of the home. Rather, the believer should do his part to keep the marriage stable. If the unbeliever is not willing to retain the relationship, the believer need not feel that he is obligated to keep the marriage intact. He may let the unbeliever go as a matter of claiming the personal peace to which God has called his people.

The source of problem for the interpreter is verse 14. The treatment of this obscure verse has caused the production of a tremendous volume of writing. Much of it is a genuine effort to clarify Paul's meaning, but more of it is representing a claim that the passage gives support to some particular view of infant baptism. The pivotal words are those which are translated as "sanctified" or "holy" and as "unclean." The first two words are renderings of the same Greek term and have exactly the same meaning. If we were able to determine with absolute certainty what Paul was saying and to express it in a current vocabulary, it is probable that the verse would still be unintelligible to most modern Baptists of this country. The concept with which he was dealing is foreign to our experience and pattern of thinking.

The words "holy" and "unclean" were used in connection with a form of ritual practices which have no part in our life. "Holy" meant that a person or thing was set apart to God, existing in some particular relationship to him or being of some particular use to him. "Unclean" is the opposite, meaning that which is unrelated to God, not usable in God's service, or unfit to approach God. Modern evangelicals tend to associate "holy" with that which is pious or moral, which meaning is impossible in this verse. To the democratic mind the idea of applying the term "unclean" to any person is repugnant.

Whether or not we understand exactly what Paul had in mind, there are some things which we may gather from the statement: (1) Neither the mate nor the children are considered to be Christian because of their family relationship to a believer. (2) The Christian is to realize that there is a value which accrues to his mate and children through their relation to him, and he is not to take that value lightly. (3) That value accrues to the other members of a Christian's family because of their relationship to the Christian, not because of what they are themselves. (4) Whatever that value may be, it is the same for the mate and for the children. (5) This is evidence that the religious faith of the husband and father did not necessarily determine the religious life of the entire family, although that practice did exercise a powerful influence in the ancient world.

Summary

In summarizing the thoughts which the New Testament expresses on our subject we can say two things: (1) Baptist faith is essentially historical, based upon the events as well as upon the teachings recorded in the Scriptures. The New Testament has been, is, and must continue to be our spiritual foundation and our primary guide in matters of teaching and practice. (2) In the problems which are encountered when dealing with the relation of children to the church we will never find the needed guidance by studying the New Testament with the purely historical view or the backward look. For reasons which we cannot know the Spirit did not lead the writers of New Testament books to record the details of what the apostolic Christians thought and practiced in this matter.

Is it possible that one reason for this may be found in a parallel situation to which the writer of Hebrews referred? After listing the heroes of the faith and pointing out they had not received the full promise of God, he said, "God having provided some better thing for us, that they without us should not be made perfect" (11:40). We have been hesitant to take seriously Jesus' promise to the disciples on his last night with them: "When he, the Spirit of truth, is come, he will guide you into all truth: for he shall not speak of himself; but whatsoever he shall hear, that shall he speak: and he will shew you things to come" (John 16:13).

There has been a tendency on the part of many to assume that the Spirit's work of revelation was completed when the Scriptures were composed and collected. There is no reason for this assumption. Jesus placed no time limit upon the Spirit's revealing work. It is as pertinent and applicable to the life of Christ's people now as it was in apostolic days. The supreme question is whether or not we are willing to allow the Spirit to lead us as a people into a fuller understanding and a more complete application of the truths which are recorded in the New Testament.

4

Problems Related to New Testament Teachings
William B. Coble

Each time man has moved into an era of broadening understanding of this physical-temporal order in which we live there has been a long period of great religious stress. Men are forced to reexamine the nature and meanings of all of life because they see everything in a new setting. The era of stress usually begins with many openly rejecting the God of the Bible as being no longer necessary to explain the nature of the world and of life.

New explanations of life's basic secrets, new standards of values, and new ways of living are produced in great abundance. Then the emptiness and inadequacies of these new results of man's thinking become inescapably evident. Then comes spiritual revival as men again humble themselves before God.

We are in the midst of the most spectacular explosion of knowledge ever experienced by man; so it is inevitable that our time be marked by intense religious turmoil. Yet we who have come to a knowledge of God in Jesus Christ live by the faith that the spiritual struggle is the prelude of an even greater spiritual renewal. How or when it will occur and what its form will be, no one knows; for God's ways are neither dependent on man nor predictable by man. Today's deep concern of people for the spiritual needs of children may be one of the preparatory movings of that renewal. The real issue before us is this: Are we willing to follow in the way that the Spirit may seek to lead us?

Whatever path we may take, two areas of beliefs commonly held among Baptists must be reexamined from the viewpoint of the New Testament itself. For a people who lay strong claims to being unbound by authoritative religious traditions, *in these two areas* we are heavily encumbered by traditions developed long after the New Testament books were written. Upon many people these traditions are so binding that they unconsciously read the Scriptures only in the light of the traditions. It may be that, as a group, our experience of spiritual renewal will be proportionate to our willingness to allow the New Testament itself to supplant the traditions. These are matters of such magnitude that an adequate treatment would require a lengthy book; so here we can only suggest the gist of the problems.

The chapter concludes with a third problem area of a different nature.

The Problem of Sin

The first area which must be reexamined is the supreme problem of human life, man's sinful nature. That the entire Bible pictures man as a sinner is beyond any question. The Scriptures show that sin permeates man's whole being and that he is helpless to remedy his own situation. This situation is often described by the postbiblical term, "total depravity." Yet with regard to the question of how man came to be in this condition, the New Testament is strangely silent.

The reason is probably found in the fact biblical writers accepted human life as it is and sought to point out the way to right handling of the problems which man meets. They did not deal in philosophical or speculative analysis of the human situation. In spite of this biblical pattern, a tradition which has its roots in speculative thought exercises a powerful influence on the thinking of many Baptists. This tradition is known as "original sin," which means that every person is born into the world a sinner *because of Adam's sin.*

Two main factors have contributed to the tradition's influence. One is the tremendous influence of Augustine (354-430), bishop of Hippo, who was one of the most powerful theologians in Christian history. He was more responsible than any other individual for the establishment of two mighty forces in Christendom, the idea of original sin and the practice of infant baptism.

The idea of spiritual regeneration by baptism had already gained wide acceptance before Augustine's time. Infant baptism had been introduced but was not widely accepted until the establishment of the idea of original sin. The three concepts, baptismal regeneration, original sin, and infant baptism fit together as naturally as the three points of a triangle and are foundation stones of Roman Catholic theology. Although Baptists have universally rejected baptismal regeneration and infant baptism, many tend to cling to some form of the idea of original sin. This strange situation has given rise to many problems in both thought and practice.

Augustine's influence has augmented the other factor which contributes to this situation. That second factor is the deep feeling that the Bible *must* provide some answer to a question which is as vital as this one: What is the cause of human sin? This feeling impels people to search the Scriptures for light on the subject; simply being engaged in the search frequently causes men to see meanings in passages which are quite different from the ideas which the writer had in mind.

The outstanding illustration of this practice is found in the handling of Romans 5:12-21, which has been the primary passage used to prove that man inherited sin and/or guilt from Adam. The idea that guilt could be inherited had been thoroughly rejected by Jeremiah and Ezekiel and has no scriptural foundation. Yet it is one of those ideas which is most tenacious in human thought.

For a true appreciation of Romans 5:12-21 one must remember that in Romans 5-7 Paul was developing a contrast between two forces which exercise rule over human life—sin and righteousness. His main points of contrast were that sin was introduced into the world through Adam, was made definite and operative by the Law, and resulted in death. Righteousness was introduced into man's life through Christ, was made operative by faith, and resulted in eternal life. The point which Paul emphasized throughout Romans 5 was the greatness of what God had done in Christ. In verses 1-11 he gave an extended statement of his theme, the wonders of justification through faith in God's great gift of love. Then in verses 12-21 Paul made use of the fact of sin, with its universal extent and deadly results, as a background against which to highlight the wondrous victory of Christ's redemptive work.

Paul's primary presentation of his view of sin is found in Romans 1:18 to 3:26. There he spelled out in detail the fact that sin is the problem of the manner of thinking and acting of the mature person, not the problem of the baby. Paul described the sinner as one who has had ample opportunity to see the reality of God's nature through the world in which he lives.

Acting with full freedom of choice, he rebels against what he knows to be true and seeks to make things be the way he wants them to be. He does this so that he may act in the way he wants to act—without the restrictions which submission to the God who created him would place upon him. In short, the essence of sin is rebellion against God as man's rightful ruler, and it occurs because man wants to act as though he were God in the world.

This concept of sin provides the light in which Romans 5:12-21 must be read. Keeping this concept in mind will eliminate the problem of trying to find in the passage a philosophical discussion of the origin of sin. It will enable one to see the fact that here sin is a backdrop for the presentation of God's righteousness as the conquest of human depravity.

Paul's method of accomplishing this purpose is a series of comparisons and/or contrasts, one each in verses 12, 16, 17, 18, 19, 20, and 21, and two in verse 15, making a total of nine in the space of ten verses. The first one sets the stage (v. 12), "Wherefore, as by one man sin entered into the world, and death by sin; and so death passed upon all men, for that all have sinned."

This comparison is of the literary style known as a chiasmus. This word is derived from the Greek letter *chi,* which was written like the capitalized form of the English letter "X." In literature it signified an expression of four points in which the first and fourth points were compared and the second and third points were compared. Refined writers made frequent use of chiasmus in both Jewish and Greek literature. Its use required some writing skill, and its presence here shows that Paul had thought out carefully what he intended to say and how he wanted to say it. This shows the falsity of an idea which some people advocate, that Paul started out to say one thing and got sidetracked before the end of the first verse. He said exactly what he had intended to say and established these two points: (1) just as sin entered humanity through one man, all men have sinned; (2) just as sin caused the death of that one man, all men have died.

In analyzing the thought of the passage its contents may be properly expressed in five steps: (1) the fact—sin entered into the world, as a force which rules over and in the life of man; (2) the agent of sin's entry—the one man, Adam; (3) the effect of sin's entry—death; (4) the extent of its effects—universal (all men); (5) the reason for the universal effects of sin—all men have sinned.

Probably the most completely ignored words in the New Testament are the closing words of Romans 5:12, "all men sinned." Exactly the same pronoun and verb begin Romans 3:23, "For all have sinned, and come short of the glory of God." (Both "sinned" and "have sinned" are proper translations of the Greek verb.) In presenting the gospel message, Baptists characteristically place great emphasis on Romans 3:23, particularly upon "all have sinned." It is fitting that we should. Yet in interpreting Romans 5:12, it is a common practice for people to act as though these words were not even in the text. Paul is then interpreted as though he had said that all men died because one man, Adam, sinned. This testifies to the power of Augustine's influence, which has lingered over a span of more than fifteen hundred years. For he said that all men were present in Adam's body (in seed form) when the first sin was committed, making all men guilty before God without any wilful act of their own. The power of tradition *can* close men's eyes and minds.

The importance of the interpretation of verse 12 is seen as one follows Paul's series of comparisons through the passage, which space will not allow us to do in detail. The matter becomes most prominent in the sixth comparison of the series, "Therefore as by the offence of one judgment came upon all men to condemnation; even so by the righteousness of one the free gift came upon all men unto justification of life" (v. 18).

If we say that Paul said that all men are guilty before God because of the act of Adam, without themselves having committed any sinful act, we *must* say that Paul said that all men are made partakers of the life which God gives in Christ without having made any response or having participated in that gift by faith. Augustine could allow this quite easily. It resulted in his conviction that the act of baptizing infants, who were totally unable to respond in faith, achieved their redemption because of what Christ had done. If we accept Augustine's doctrine of original sin, how can we maintain *both* the glory of divine grace and the practice of a strict believer's baptism? If we say that a child is innocent or is safe (*not* saved) until he reaches that age at which he becomes accountable to God for the choices which he makes, we do not accept the doctrine of original sin in its true meaning.

The fifth comparison of the series most clearly expresses the thought of the whole argument, "For if by one man's offence death reigned by one; much more they which receive abundance of grace and of the gift of righteousness shall reign in life by one, Jesus Christ" (v. 17). This is the main point to which Paul moved in a step-by-step development, beginning with the fact of sin's entry into human life as a power which rules and destroys man's life. It concludes with the wondrous fact that sin and its effects are overcome by God's righteousness as a power which also rules in human existence and brings man eternal life.

The message of the passage is the glorious victory which God, in the righteousness of Jesus Christ, has won over sin and death. So the origin and nature of sin is not the main theme (that was found in Romans 1:18 to 3:26). But the idea of sin plays the part of the supporting role, making it possible to see clearly the nature of the victory by specifying the enemy which has been defeated.

Another significant item comes from this passage, but it is not as easy to pinpoint as is the problem of sin and its nature. This is the idea that the work of Christ has redeemed the entire human race. One's position on the idea hinges largely on his interpretation of verse 18: "Therefore as by the offence of one judgment came upon all men to condemnation; even so by the righteousness of one the free gift came upon all men unto justification of life."

In a similar statement Paul said, "For since by man came death, by man came also the resurrection of the dead. For as in Adam all die, even so in Christ shall all be made alive" (1 Cor. 15:21-22). There are those interpreters who say that this was what Paul had intended to say in Romans 5:12ff, but that he got sidetracked; so what Paul meant to be setting out in Romans 5:12-21 was a universal redemption in Christ which is parallel to the universal experience of death in Adam.

It is interesting to remember, however, that 1 Corinthians was written before Romans, and that Paul was in Corinth when he wrote Romans. It may be that Paul found that the brief, concise statement in 1 Corinthians was more confusing than enlightening; so he found it necessary to make a more complete statement to avoid the very idea which these people wish to read into Romans. There can be no question that in 1 Corinthians 15:22 there is a simple equation, "as in Adam, death for all; even so in Christ, life for all."

Yet at no point in Paul's writings nor in his preaching recorded in Acts is there the slightest suggestion that God has purposed to redeem men apart from their response of faith. This is stated categorically in Romans 5:17, "They which receive abundance of grace and of the gift of righteousness shall reign in life by one, Jesus Christ." Paul assumed that Christ died *for* all men, but the saving efficacy of his death is limited by the voluntary response of men. Also the stress of Romans 5:12-21 is that the free gift of life in Christ is *not* like the effect of the act of Adam; it is far greater. "Much more" is the theme, rather than "even so" (cf. vv. 15-17, 20).

The point of all of this for us is simply that Paul was describing the practical situation which prevails in adult life. He was *not* giving a philosophical statement of the condition into which babies are born and in which young children live. This should have a distinct effect upon our views of child evangelism. Many Baptists show that their concern over preschoolers and children stems from the suspicion that these little ones were born sinners. Yet in presenting the New Testament message to small children we face at least three problems: (1) The New Testament vocabulary of sin represents acts which are essentially adult in nature. The vast majority of the words are utterly meaningless to the preteen child. Therefore, if we try to make a small child to feel guilty for and repent of something which he lacks even the personal maturity to comprehend, we may be doing something which is harmful to the child's entire personality, as well as to his view of God.

(2) Sin is a problem at the center of man's nature, not just at the end of his fingers; so he needs a new "heart," not a new skin. Yet being given a new heart can have meaning only to one who is sufficiently mature to be able to exercise the freedom of choosing for himself. There are many reasons for doubting the ability of a child to do this when he has just begun the search for himself and as yet has not achieved the slightest idea of who or what he really is. (3) Repentance is the act of a person who is mature enough to be able to recognize that something—an attitude, a thought, or an act—is devastating to his own being. Until he can see this, repentance is just a word; it can never be an experience.

These are just a few reasons, based upon a New Testament approach to sin, why Baptist evangelistic fervor for small children needs to be thoroughly reexamined. Are we winning those who are lost to a saving faith in Christ? Or are we giving to innocents a religious inoculation which will make it even more difficult for saving grace to enter their life and overcome the invading power of sin, once they have become conscious of its operation?

The Meaning of Salvation

Another area in which some Baptist thinking has produced grave problems can be illustrated by many experiences. A pastor told of having urged his young son to wait for baptism after the boy had told him that he had put his faith in Christ. After the meeting in which the story was related, the pastor was accosted by a number of people, all Baptists. One woman was particularly heated and asked, "Well, just what would you have done if that boy had died before *you* let him be baptized?"

A Sunday School teacher urged all of his class of nine-year-old boys to go forward at the morning's closing service of a revival meeting in their church, saying to them, "If you should die before you accept Jesus, you would go to hell." He was like the evangelist who spoke at an associational meeting on the subject of the use of the Sunday School in the promotion of a simultaneous evangelistic crusade. He said, "Get all the kids from the little ones to the big ones back there together, *without* the teachers; and I *mean, put the pressure on!*" When asked why he would use his method, he said, "I'm willing to do anything I have to do to keep people out of hell."

In his own way each of those three persons represents a view which is common in Baptist life, and usually those who are of such persuasion feel that they alone are faithful to the New Testament. Commendable as such concern may seem to be on the surface, deeper examination will show that it involves at least two drastic departures from central emphases of the New Testament. One is found in the view of God which is manifested. It is one which is derived, at least most recently, from Puritan influence. God is viewed as a fiercely angry being whose main purpose is to see that every person receives the full measure of punishment which is due him.

The New Testament leaves no reasonable room for doubt that man must someday face divine judgment. Yet the function of this truth is to provide the constant background for the presentation of the gospel. *The good news:* "God so loved the world, that he gave his only begotten Son" (John 3:16), that God sent not his Son—to condemn —but to save, and "God commendeth his love toward us, in that, while we were yet sinners, Christ died for us" (Rom. 5:8). God has done and is doing everything possible to bring life to mankind. He is not engaged in a form of eternal "brinkmanship" in an effort to see how many of the young and unwary he can trap into damnation.

Of course, the practical problem must be faced: the time does arrive when persons become subject to judgment, which problem is discussed by Dr. William Hendricks in chapter 6 of this book. This is one of the matters on which we must do much diligent study, for there is so little that we know about it. Yet in making the study our spirit should be that of trustful submission to the guidance of the God who, in unlimited love, purposes to redeem those for whom we are concerned, rather than that of nagging doubts and of fear of his punishment.

The second great weakness of the statements of the three persons is found in their view of Christ's salvation as a work which determines only one's fate after physical death, deliverance from the condemnation of hell, and the guarantee of reward in heaven. Although the anticipation of blessing beyond the grave is a part of the total scope of salvation as set out in the New Testament, it is far from being the whole picture, or even the most important part of it. In both Testaments the words translated as "save" and "salvation" express two basic ideas—deliverance from danger and the providing of fulness or completeness of life. The second meaning is by far the more important and the more often used of the two, particularly in the New Testament. Too, in New Testament expression the term "eternal life" meant far more than everlasting existence of life or endless duration.

The King James Version is largely responsible for establishing in modern minds the idea that eternal is a synonym for everlasting. In the New Testament "eternal life" meant a life of a distinctive quality, the kind of life which one can experience only in a living relationship with God. The nearest thing we have to a definition is found in John 17:3, "This is life eternal, that they might know thee the only true God, and Jesus Christ, whom thou hast sent."

"Know" means to have the knowledge which is the result of direct, personal association. Paul's most characteristic term for expressing the same idea is to be "in Christ." This does not describe a status but defines an experience of life fellowship. That experience is marked by several qualities which make the life of the person distinctly different from the life of those who have not been introduced to it.

Three of them stand out for special consideration: (1) The indwelling presence of the Holy Spirit, as Paul said, "If any man have not the Spirit of Christ, he is none of his. . . . For as many as are led by the Spirit of God, they are the sons of God" (Rom. 8:9-14).

(2) An awareness of one's own place in the Christian mission, which is probably most clearly stated in Jesus' invitation to Simon Peter and his brother Andrew, "Come ye after me, and I will make you to become fishers of men" (Mark 1:17). Although these two men did become apostles at a later time, nothing was involved in the invitation which was extended to them at the beginning of their discipleship which is not involved in any person's acceptance of Jesus Christ. Jesus was speaking of all of his followers when he said, "As my Father hath sent me, even so send I you" (John 20:21).

(3) Participation in a fellowship of mutual love and upbuilding. At no point does the New Testament countenance the idea of either the secret follower or the "lone wolf" disciple. The church is the natural result of the kind of fellowship which exists among believers. It is only in such a joint relationship that Christian believers can experience the growth and render the service which is the expression of life in Christ.

Although many other matters are involved in the question of the nature of salvation offered in the New Testament, these are at the center. As we seek to lead children to accept Jesus Christ, we must face the question of just how much of this type of experience they are capable of knowing. This writer can present no ready nor easy answers to the multitude of problems which are connected with that question.

But we must realize that the kind of experience which the New Testament offers man is probably poles apart from the thing which a child has in mind when he stands before a congregation and silently nods his assent to the question, "Do you love Jesus and want to follow him?" One college student said, "I was accepted into the church on that very statement, and they had just as well have asked me if I loved Panky (her toy panda); it would have meant the same thing to me. And following Jesus just meant going to Sunday School when I felt like it." Although it is *not* our job to keep people out of the kingdom of God and out of the church, it *is* our job to do everything possible to see that all people, especially our children, are fully aware of the meaning of the Christian faith before they go through the motions of accepting it. In this effort we *must* be true to the New Testament, for only then can we be true to God and to the people whom Christ died to save.

The Question of Household Baptisms

A large percentage of Baptists in America are unaware of the fact that there are highly able scholars—dedicated Christians—who are convinced that the New Testament teaches infant baptism and that New Testament Christians practiced it. One of the major pillars of their conviction is known as "household baptisms." The idea is based upon the essential unity of the home under the father as the head. This meant that whatever he did automatically included the entire household.

The New Testament tells us of six specific cases of a person and his (her) house or whole house believing or being baptized: (1) The nobleman whose son, who was in Capernaum, was healed by Jesus when he was in Cana. The father, after hearing of the healing, "himself believed, and his whole house" (John 4:53). In keeping with the purpose and method of John's Gospel (cf. 20:30-31) we are told no more about him.

(2) Cornelius was the centurion of Caesarea, about whose experience several statements are found. He is described as "one that feared God with all his house" (Acts 10:2). Simon Peter in his report of his experience before the elders in Jerusalem, included the angelic messenger's statement to Cornelius, "Send men to Joppa, and call for Simon, whose surname is Peter; who shall tell thee words, whereby thou and all thy house shall be saved" (Acts 11:13-14). In interpreting this entire story, it is common for people to overlook two statements which are recorded in Acts 10: "The morrow after they entered into Caesarea. And Cornelius waited for them, and had called together his kinsmen and near friends" (v. 24); and "While Peter yet spake these words, the Holy Ghost fell on all them which heard the word" (v. 44). It is difficult to see how Luke's purpose in making this report could have been other than to indicate that those who were involved were adults.

(3) Lydia, the merchant of Philippi, is described as one who, "when she was baptized, and her household" (Acts 16:15), persuaded the apostles to stay in her home. (4) The Philippian jailer, who asked, "Sirs, what must I do to be saved?" (Acts 16:30). Both the answer and the ensuing story contain several references to the household, "They said, Believe on the Lord Jesus Christ, and thou shalt be saved, and thy house. And they spake unto him the word of the Lord, and to all that were in his house. And he took them the same hour of the night, and washed their stripes; and was baptized, he and all his, straightway. And when he had brought them into his house, he set meat before them, and rejoiced, believing in God with all his house" (Acts 16:31-34).

It is not insignificant that Luke recorded that, not only was the whole household baptized, but also the whole household heard the word of the Lord and the whole household rejoiced because the whole household had put their faith in God.

(5) Crispus, the ruler of the synagogue in Corinth, is described as having "believed on the Lord with all his house; and many of the Corinthians hearing believed, and were baptized" (Acts 18:8). (6) Stephanas, of whom Paul said, "I baptized also the household of Stephanas" (1 Cor. 1:16), and "Now, brethren, you know that the household of Stephanas were the first converts in Achaia, and they have devoted themselves to the service of the saints" (1 Cor. 16:15, RSV). It is difficult to see how any consistence can be maintained between these two statements without assuming that the household of Stephanas was a group of adults.

These are the passages upon which advocates of infant baptism must base the primary weight of their case for New Testament support for their practice. Yet five of the six households are described as having a kind of experience such as the New Testament attributes to adults. The Capernaum official, the Philippian jailer, and Crispus are described as believing. The Holy Spirit came upon those who were in Cornelius' house, and the household of Stephanas was dedicated to the service of the saints. So only the household of Lydia is actually open to the kind of thinking which the defenders of infant baptism must adopt. They say it is reasonable to assume that some of the households included some small children, and these must have been baptized when the whole household was baptized.

Some scholars justify this assumption by citing the results of intensive study of the term "he and his whole house" and kindred expressions in the Old Testament and in early Greek writings. A strong case can be made for the position that the term characteristically was used to include small children. See, for example, the two small books on infant baptism by Joachim Jeremias. Since the term was used in that way in both the Old Testament and in the Greek writings, and since the New Testament says nothing to indicate that this meaning is not to be applied to the expression, they insist that we must assume that these families included small children and that they were baptized along with the adults.

Baptists have always rejected such arguments and insisted that the New Testament speaks only of believer's baptism. Many prominent scholars who are affiliated with groups who practice infant baptism have acknowledged that the New Testament itself provides no basis for their church's practice. Yet while we continue to reject their interpretation and their practice, we must remember one often overlooked truth: baptizing infants is an effort to bridge a great gap between the Old and New Testaments. This gap has produced many serious problems for Christians throughout the ages, including the very problems which have made this study necessary.

To appreciate the nature of the gap between the Testaments one must give serious consideration to several elements of life in the Old Testament covenant community as they are discussed in chapter 2 of this book, written by Dr. Roy L. Honeycutt, Jr. Particular thought must be given to the idea of corporate unity. This concept meant that an Israelite's son was a member of the covenant community simply because of his physical descent from a member of that community. The idea of corporate unity had many implications, some good and some bad.

Dr. Honeycutt has described some of the problems, particularly as they related to the ministry and message of Jeremiah and Ezekiel. The tendency to carry to extremes the implications of that unity forced those prophets to make forcible statements of personal responsibility before God, that the individual's relation to God is determined by his own conduct, not by who his family is nor by what his family has done. Even so, to both Jeremiah and Ezekiel the foundation of that person's standing before God was still the fact that he was a member of the covenant community of Israel. Thus each person knew of his own standing in relation to the other members of that community.

Paul insisted that life under the old covenant was the life of a child who was being prepared for the mature life which comes to the individual in the voluntary exercise of his own faith in Christ (cf. Gal. 3:24 to 4:6). The letter to the Hebrews shows that the covenant which was promised in Jeremiah 31:31-34 was fulfilled in Christ, who provided a far better covenant than the old one (Heb. 8:6-13; 10:15-18). Baptists insist that only those who respond to God's gracious offer in Christ with the submissive obedience of faith have entered into the new covenant of which Jesus said, "This is my blood of the [*mg.* new] covenant" (Matt. 26:28, RSV).

Thus no one's entry into this covenant relationship is in any way automatic; he cannot just back into it by choosing the right parents nor receive a place in the covenant by proxy. In Baptist eyes this is a matter of great value, for it means that only those who choose to do so can enter into that relationship. For adults this is most meaningful.

Yet in spite of the strength which comes from these convictions, there is a real problem: *What about the children?* Although the child attends worship gatherings and business meetings, until he professes publicly that he has submitted himself to Christ's lordship in faith, he is only a spectator in the life and work of the church. He is not forced to remain outside the church; yet, while he is on the inside of the building, he is still just looking in on what transpires there. There is a sense in which a young child is in a Christian family, but he is not really one of that Christian family.

Under the old covenant such a problem did not exist, and infant baptism has been an effort to eliminate it from the new covenant. Some base their defense of infant baptism upon the fact that the new covenant grew directly out of the old, resulting in an inherent unity between the two covenants. Since family unity was essential to the old covenant, they feel that it is folly to suppose that such unity was not a part of the life and practice of those who had entered the new, especially the Jewish Christians; so the children of believers are born within the covenant of grace.

The strong point of this position is that the child, in fact the whole community of faith, lives under the awareness that children are an essential part of that life—*as children,* not as little or undeveloped adults. The great weakness of the view is that it tends to overlook the difference between God's grace as shown in the old covenant and as shown in the new.

When Israel was chosen to be a special people, grace meant that favor was extended to those who merely had no legitimate claim to special treatment. The nation was in a condition of nonmerit which provided no reason to expect the establishment of a unique relationship (cf. Deut. 4:37; 6:6-8); but grace established it. In the new covenant grace is the extension of God's forgiveness and transforming power to those who have positively rejected him and violated a recognized relationship. As Paul said: "God shows his love for us in that while we were yet sinners Christ died for us" (Rom. 5:8, RSV).

Although most groups which practice infant baptism do not make the small child a full-fledged participant in the community of grace, bringing infants into the body leaves no place for the operation of that which makes the new covenant distinctive, the experience which most evangelicals call "conversion." The special nature of the life in Christ is the realization that God has come to one after he has failed to live up to what he knows he should be, when he has become aware of his own failure and of his inability to act in accord with the standards of which he himself approves.

The forgiveness extended to him in that experience enables him to know God as he never could have known him before he became aware of his failures, no matter how much a part of the covenant community he may have been. Without that experience of personal repentance and the redirection of faith one can never know the full meaning of the new covenant.

It is at this point that modern Baptists, particularly Southern Baptists, are introducing a solution which many feel to be another form of infant baptism. Our effort to bridge the gap between the covenants has taken the form of seeking to evangelize children at age levels which are being lowered constantly. The major difference between this and the action of groups which have practiced infant baptism for centuries is that our preschoolers, upon their baptism, are made full-fledged members of an essentially adult fellowship. This practice is now producing at least two results: (1) We have large numbers of utterly baffled children who are trying to act out a part which they clearly do not understand; (2) We have ever-growing numbers of young people who are saying, "When I joined the church, I didn't know what I was doing; I hadn't the slightest idea of what it was all about."

We cannot escape the accompanying question: Is it possible that this same situation is the primary reason for the equally growing number of young people who completely separate themselves from the church and all for which it stands? Do they *think* that they have experienced all that Christ offers and have found it meaningless, when in reality they have experienced *nothing* while going through some standardized motions? These are questions with which we must begin coming to grips.

5

Historic Practices Regarding Children
Hugh Wamble

The purpose of this chapter is to offer evidence from Christian history on varied theories and practices relating to the admission of children into the church. It deals with baptism, confirmation, and instruction.

Early Church

Christian literature of the first two centuries offers little information about the church's practice involving children. However, two generalizations may be made.

First, early Christians included children in their gatherings—as attenders, not as formal members of the church. Christians differed from other religious groups in the Roman empire by taking children to their meetings. Some opponents falsely accused Christians of eating human flesh, particularly the flesh of young children, in their secret meetings. This charge derived from a misunderstanding of the Lord's Supper (including "body" and "blood"). Refuting the charge of cannibalism, Christians appealed to their respect for life and to their condemnation of abortion, murder, and child-exposure.

Second, early Christians baptized neither infants nor young children. Literature predating A.D. 200 contains no reference to infant baptism. The evidence in this literature suggests adult baptism as the normal practice. The earliest Christian manual on this subject, entitled *Didache* (meaning "teaching") and dated around 110-125, called for converts to learn Christianity's moral teachings before

71

undergoing baptism. Around 150 a person was baptized only after he accepted Christianity's theological and moral teachings as true and pledged to live according to Christian standards. By 200 converts customarily repeated a trinitarian creed and renounced the devil at the time of baptism.

During the third century, prebaptismal instruction and probation lasted up to three years. The candidate, called a catechumen (meaning "an instructed person"), received careful instruction in Christian doctrine (including the Trinity, creation, judgment) and in what it means to renounce the devil. Catechumens were excluded from some parts of Christian worship, especially the Lord's Supper. Communion was a privilege of baptized Christians only.

Infant Baptism and Original Sin

Child baptism arose during the third century. Tertullian (died around 225) of Carthage, the so-called "father of Latin Christianity," was the first to mention it. But he opposed it. He cautioned against baptizing "young novices" because, though they can recite the right words, they are unable either to repent or to understand what it means to live a life of repentance. Tertullian opposed baptizing "little children" during the "innocent period of life"; he preferred that baptism be delayed until one had passed through the heat of youth.

By 250, however, infant baptism was practiced, particularly in North Africa around Carthage. A minor controversy developed over when to baptize infants. Some favored postponing baptism for two or three days after birth due to "impurity" incurred during delivery. Cyprian (died 258), bishop of Carthage, favored baptizing infants immediately after birth—for several reasons. (1) No one, including infants, should be refused God's mercy and grace. (2) God bestows his grace equally on all, whether infants or older persons. (3) An infant bears a fresh image of God, and therefore "impurity" incurred in birth is not an "impediment" to grace.

(4) Hebrew sons were circumcised on the eighth day, but the children of Christians should be baptized on the day of birth, for the Jewish eighth day is the first Christian day. (5) If baptism can remit the gross sins of adults, it can certainly remit the sin of infancy—namely, Adam's sin. (6) The first sound made by an infant is his urgent plea for divine mercy through baptism.

Two ideas led to infant baptism: (1) In the second century baptism came to be viewed as a means of washing sins away. Before 150 *The Shepherd of Hermas* suggested that baptism washes away sins committed prior to baptism. Baptism came to be viewed as essential to salvation, except in the case of martyrs. Martyrdom, Tertullian held, stands in the place of water-baptism.

(2) In the third century, the doctrine of original sin made it imperative for infants to receive baptism. And original sin became the chief justification for infant baptism for several centuries. Cyprian affirmed that infants contract from Adam the contagion of the ancient death, but he held that an infant has not sinned, except in that he has been affected by "the sins of another."

What Cyprian suggested, Augustine (354-430), bishop of Hippo in North Africa, developed into a full blown rationale for infant baptism. He viewed baptism as the remedy for original sin.

This is Augustine's basic view: Created morally good, Adam sinned, and his nature became corrupt. All of his posterity share his corrupt nature, for all members of the human race were seminally present when Adam sinned. All are guilty and are justly punished with death. Original sin is a condition deriving from Adam, inherited by all of his descendants, and punished by death.

Baptism is God's instrument for remitting sins and regenerating sinners. Without baptism neither adult nor infant is eternally saved. In the case of adults, baptism remits both original sin and actual sins committed between birth and baptism. In the case of infants, baptism remits original sin only, for infants are not yet guilty of personal, actual sin. An infant dying without baptism cannot avoid condemnation, but he faces a mild condemnation. Augustine contended that anyone who denies original sin has no reason to baptize infants.

Confirmation

For centuries confirmation has been associated with admitting children to certain privileges. Its origin is unknown. Historians' suggestion that it evolved from anointing with oil and laying on of hands is not too helpful.

Laying hands on newly baptized persons apparently disappeared after the New Testament era (Acts 8:17). By 200, however Christians again practiced it. And by this time anointing with oil also followed baptism. North African Christians regarded anointing as essential to a valid baptism by 250. Cyprians held that only the church, acting through the bishop, can sanctify the oil used in anointing. The Council of Carthage (258) regarded laying on of hands as essential to the gift of the Spirit. Since the Spirit operates only in the mainstream Church, the council reasoned, each Christian must undergo laying on of hands in the Church.

During the third century, the catechumenate, consisting of persons preparing for baptism, appeared in the Eastern church. During a period of probation, lasting up to three years, the catechumen received instruction in the faith. The catechumenate became more common during the fourth century. The Synod of Laodicea (around 363) ordered that "they who are baptized must after Baptism be anointed with the heavenly chrism, and be partakers of the Kingdom of Christ" (canon 48). The Council of Carthage (419) forbade presbyters to administer chrism (oil) to penitents, presumably because only bishops could do this. The foregoing evidence relates to older persons, not to infants.

Middle Ages: Orthodoxy and Roman Catholicism

Infant baptism became a more frequent practice after 400, but believer's baptism remained the most common practice for several centuries. Various councils ordered the immediate baptism of infants to insure that they gain the cleansing value of baptism. Various regulations applied to the baptism of infants who had no relatives to stand witness and of children too young to give satisfactory statements of faith.

Eastern Orthodoxy observed three sacraments until the seventeenth century: baptism, chrismation (chrism), and eucharist. According to its definitive theologian, John of Damascus (died 754), baptism remits sins and confers eternal life (deification). Chrismation, successor to the ancient practice of anointing with olive oil after baptism, announces or signifies God's pity in relieving man's urgent need.

Western theologians, beginning in the mid-eleventh century, listed seven sacraments: baptism, confirmation, penance, eucharist, marriage, ordination, and extreme unction. The person who fixed seven as the number of sacraments was Peter the Lombard (died around 1160). Thomas Aquinas (1225-1275) developed and the Council of Trent (1547) adopted the sacramental theology now held by Roman Catholics.

The chief features of Thomas Aquinas's view are: Sacraments are means of grace and necessary for salvation. Man sinned, and God instituted sacraments to correct defects caused by sin and to perfect man in worship of God. Original sin harms one's soul, not his flesh. Baptism regenerates and remedies man's soul and enables him to worship God. Infant baptism, administered shortly after birth, signifies washing away uncleanness deriving from Adam. It removes only the guilt of original sin; it does not remove or remedy a corrupted nature which passes from parents to child. Therefore, when a Christian marries and has children, his children are subject to original sin and must undergo baptism to remove the guilt attached to original sin.

Baptism, according to Thomas Aquinas, is the sacrament of spiritual birth or regeneration; confirmation, the sacrament of maturity. Confirmation, like baptism, confers an indelible character and is therefore irrepeatable. When a person baptized in infancy reaches "the perfect age" he undergoes confirmation, the final completion of the sacrament of baptism. Administered only by bishops, confirmation confers the Holy Spirit, stimulates growth, and strengthens the believer.

The age at which Roman Catholic children receive confirmation has varied. The catechism approved by the Council of Trent indicates twelve as the age of preconfirmation instruction. Seven has been the minimal age of confirmation since 1931, but most children are older when confirmed.

Lutheranism

Most major wings of Protestantism—Lutheran, Reformed, Presbyterian, Anglican, and Congregational—retained infant baptism but offered differing explanations of it. Beginning with Luther (1483-1546) in 1519, all Protestants rejected the Roman Catholic idea that sacraments convey grace, reduced the number of sacraments to two (baptism and Lord's Supper), and proposed new explanations.

Luther gave baptism a central place in his doctrine of the Church. He regarded faith as essential to baptism, and he viewed baptism as "an exercise of faith" which focuses on Jesus' death and resurrection. Despite this emphasis, however, Luther urged that infants be baptized because baptism aids infants—not directly through the act, but indirectly through the faith of those who bring them to baptism.

If God's power can change the "godless heart" of an adult, he argued, it can change an infant's heart.

Luther originally made no provision for confirmation, for he denied that Roman Catholic Confirmation is a sacrament. However, he recognized the need of instructing youth. In 1529, he introduced a catechism for educating youth on the Ten Commandments, Apostles' Creed, Lord's Prayer, baptism, confession, Lord's Supper, private prayers, and other duties. In practice, ministers privately examined children who had received instruction and admitted them to communion. Lutherans have explained confirmation variously: as an ending of instruction and renewal of baptismal pledge, as certification that a baptized child has come of age, as a means of receiving a youth into an adult congregation where he may enjoy communion (Lord's Supper), as a supplement to baptism, and as a means of conferring the Holy Spirit. They have developed a uniform practice of confirmation. At an "accountable age"—usually between ten and fifteen years —a child who has learned the catechism makes a public profession, undergoes the laying on of hands, and receives the Lord's Supper.

Reformed Tradition

Zwingli (1484-1531) went further than Luther in defending infant baptism. He came to believe that infant baptism is essential to preserving a state church. He became the first opponent of rebaptism (anabaptism). Zwingli denied that baptism has cleansing power and that infant baptism removes the guilt of original sin. Each person comes into the world with a weakness to sin, he held, but this weakness does not carry guilt. He viewed baptism as an initiatory sign or pledge with which Christians bind themselves to God. Infant baptism is the sign of the new covenant, as circumcision was the sign of the old covenant.

Calvin (1509-1564), major systematic theologian of the Reformed-Presbyterian tradition, developed the doctrine of infant baptism which became normative for English evangelicals practicing it. His basic principle was: A sacrament is an "outward sign by which the Lord seals" his promises and sustains a Christian's faith. Baptism signifies initiation into God's church. Fundamentally, Calvin held, baptism is the seal of the covenant, analogous to circumcision.

Under the old covenant, infants were circumcised even though they did not know the meaning of circumcision. Under the new covenant, infants are to undergo baptism unto future repentance and faith, for, as infants, they do not know repentance and faith. Infant baptism carries two blessings: (1) it gives to believing parents "a surer confidence because they see the covenant of the Lord engraved upon the bodies of their children," and (2) it engrafts children "into the body of the church" and serves to spur them to zealous worship of God when they grow up. Like all evangelicals, Calvin held that an unbaptized adult who is converted to Christianity is to be baptized on the basis of his personal repentance and faith.

Calvin favored a ceremony for children who complete the catechism, but he too repudiated the Roman Catholic sacrament of confirmation. He provided for instructing children with a catechism and then, at the end of their childhood on the beginning of adolescence, of calling on each to make a public confession of faith.

Anglicanism

Anglicanism perpetuated the distinction between infant and adult baptism and gave confirmation its most prominent place among Protestants. Since the Anglican *Book of Common Prayer* (1549-62) has exerted much influence in England and America, its liturgy deserves special consideration. The liturgy of infant baptism requires that godparents (sponsors), acting in a child's behalf, take a vow assenting to doctrines of the Apostles' Creed and pledging to abide in the Christian faith.

The minister affirms that the child, after baptism, "is regenerate, and grafted into the body of Christ's Church." Also, the minister reminds the sponsors of their "parts and duties to see that *this Infant* be taught basic christian doctrines, so soon as *he* shall be able to learn." Anglicans also provided for the baptism of adults on the basis of a personal confession, without the aid of a sponsor.

The Church of England provides only one catechism "to be learned by every person before he be brought to be confirmed by the bishop." At a "competent" age—originally twelve to sixteen, but now ten to twelve, or lower—baptized and catechized children are presented, by a minister, to a bishop for confirmation that he may lay hands on them. The bishop asks if the candidates "renew the solemn promise and vow that ye made, or that was made in your name, at your Baptism." If they ratify and confirm the vow, he lays hands on each candidate's head, and prays that God will enable the candidates to continue in the Holy Spirit. Lord's Supper follows confirmation.

Infant Baptism and Covenant Theology

English and Scottish Calvinists of the seventeenth century, going beyond Calvin's emphasis on covenant, developed a doctrinal system known in history as Covenant Theology. Its basic emphasis was the inclusion of all Christians' children in a covenant relation with God, similar to the relation in Abraham's covenant.

Presbyterians and Congregationalists agreed on covenant theology but disagreed over the practical use of the seal (baptism). Presbyterians held that the external seal may be given to the children of all church members. Congregationalists held that it may be given to children of believing parents only.

The church covenant, basic to Congregationalism, developed in keeping with a Covenant Theology. Congregationalists taught that a visible, particular church is a society of believers joined together by a covenant. All members should be regenerate persons. The church consists of believers and their children, for the covenant of the grace includes children as well as adults. Being in the covenant, children should receive its seal—baptism.

Covenantal unity between believing parent and child is the basis of infant baptism. It prevents the baptism of children whose parents are outside of the covenant. Until nonbelieving parents profess repentance and faith and are baptized, they are outside of the covenant; if they are without grace, their children cannot inherit it. Baptized infants are not "perfect members" of the church, and they may not exercise acts of communion until they can show "an increase of faith." The Lord's Supper is open only to those of age who are visibly capable of nourishment and growth in the Church.

According to Congregational doctrine, a person baptized in infancy should "own the covenant" when "grown up unto years of discretion." After a "trial and examination" and "an open profession" of faith and repentance, one is given the privileges of communion. Baptism makes one a church member; owning the covenant makes him a communing member.

The doctrine did not work perfectly. Some, unable to demonstrate faith and repentance, failed voluntarily to "own the covenant." This created a problem for New England Congregationalists. Practical questions arose. Does failure to own the covenant result in loss of membership? Are children of parents baptized in infancy but not owning the covenant later to be baptized? New England Congregationalists developed a half-way covenant to keep in the church persons baptized in infancy who failed to own the covenant. It permitted the baptizing of an infant of one whose grandparent was in full communion but whose parent, though baptized, had not actually owned the covenant on his personal faith.

Puritans attacked Anglican confirmation on the ground that it detracts from the two sacraments instituted by Christ (baptism and the Lord's Supper). But they catechetically instructed children. Presbyterians' *The Book of Discipline* (1587) recommended two catechisms (larger and shorter). The shorter catechism called for a monthly examination of faith and morals as prerequisite to communion and forbade admitting children "to the Communion before they be of the age of 14 years" unless they satisfy elders and deacons. The Westminster (Presbyterian) Shorter Catechism (1648) became one of the most influential documents in the English-speaking world before the twentieth century. Both Congregationalists and Baptists adapted it to their needs. Catechisms declined in usefulness shortly around 1900 due to new means of religious education (*e.g.,* Sunday Schools) and to a new philosophy of education (as developed by John Dewey) critical of instruction requiring memorization.

Presbyterian and Congregationalists have traditionally observed a special service for admitting baptized children to communion. Presbyterians originally called it "the rite of admission to full membership," but no term is standard at present. Among American Presbyterians there is considerable variety as to age and procedure. In preparing children for communion, through a "communicants' class," most now use the Westminster Shorter Catechism. At the age of accountability or age of decision—variously placed from ten to sixteen—"children of the covenant" are admitted to communion through a simple service in which they personally answer questions about their faith.

Most Congregationalists now conduct a class—called "pastor's class" or "confirmation"—lasting from a few weeks (during Lent, for example) to a year. At the conclusion, children are admitted to communion through a simple ceremony. The age of admission to communion has been around thirteen. Congregationalists tend to make a distinction between communion and voting. They permit communicant children to vote on spiritual matters but not on legal matters until they come of legal age.

"Gathered Church" and Believer's Baptism

Some evangelicals, both on the Continent and in England, favored the "gathered church," consisting of baptized and disciplined believers only.

The continental movement first arose in 1525 among Zwingli's followers in Switzerland. Called Anabaptists (rebaptizers) by their opponents because they baptized believers who had already received baptism in infancy, they called themselves "Brethren." They are now known as Mennonites. Though rejecting infant baptism, they retained the Zwinglian-Calvinist view that baptism is the means by which one enters the covenant of grace and is incorporated into the church.

Anabaptists repudiated infant baptism for several reasons: Christ did not institute it; children can neither understand gospel-preaching nor make a decision of faith; infant baptism confuses the church with the world; and, as held by some but not all, Adam's descendants are born without the guilt of original sin and therefore do not need baptism at birth.

Anabaptists originally understood believer's baptism to permit only the baptizing of persons who hear the gospel, voluntarily accept it, and give evidence of conversion and upright living. Most European Mennonite groups baptized none under fifteen to eighteen years of age, but in Holland the minimal age was twenty. Under the influence of revivalism, American Mennonites have tended to baptize at a younger age—around ten to twelve. They also adopted the pattern of other revivalistic groups and now baptize converts a few weeks after conversion, following rudimentary instruction.

The English movement, historically known as Baptist, originated within Puritanism. Particular Baptists held Calvinistic views on sin and grace associated with the definitions of the Synod of Dort (1618-19), and General Baptists held Armenian views on sin and grace condemned at Dort.

Seven London Baptist congregations issued a confession in 1644 based on the Congregational (Separatist) *A True Confession of the Faith* (1596) but altered at some points of doctrine and practice.

In 1677 Particular Baptists used the Presbyterian Westminster

Confession (1646) as the basis of their statement. This in America is known as the Philadelphia Confession (1742) and became the most influential American statement before the Civil War. It used Westminster words and articles, except where they differed from Presbyterians. Baptism is a sign of fellowship with Christ's death and resurrection, of being engrafted into him, of remission of sin, and of a commitment to live and walk in newness of Life. The only proper subjects are persons who do actually profess repentance towards *God,* faith in, and obedience to our Lord Jesus, and dipping is necessary to the due administration of this ordinance.

Baptists accepted the theory of congregational government but differed from Congregationalists over the church's constituency. Holding that a self-governing church consists of saints and their children, Congregationalists baptized both believers and their children. Baptists, however, insisted that the church consists of saints only, not of saints and their children; so, they baptized believers only. Baptists came under attack from Calvinistic paedobaptists (Anglican, Presbyterian, and Congregationalist) who charged Baptists with hating children and depriving them of salvation by withholding the covenant's seal from them.

Baptists developed two different theories regarding the security of dying infants, a crucial issue raised by their opponents. First, General Baptists held that, since infants are not damned by virtue of original sin, their security is not impaired if they die without baptism. John Smyth (died 1612), inaugurator of believer's baptism among English refugees in Holland, said: "We pronounce nothing of dying infants, but leave the secret of them to the Lord." John Murton (died around 1625), successor to Thomas Helwys as leader of the first Baptist congregation on English soil, went further than Smyth. Murton denied original sin and affirmed that "no Infant whatsoever is in the estate of condemnation of Hell with the wicked." Thomas Grantham, most prolific writer among second-generation General Baptists, wrote more on the subject than any other Baptist. He affirmed original sin but denied that it leads to infant damnation, since infants have neither "a capacity to believe, nor any liberty to choose."

Second, Particular Baptists based their self-styled charitable opinion concerning dying infants on divine election and sufficiency of Christ's satisfaction. They appealed to the Calvinistic view that the salvation of all persons—infants or others, whether they have heard the gospel or not—rests on God's electing grace and the Spirits' work. If only elect persons are saved, as Calvinists believed, only elect infants are saved. If salvation rests on God's electing grace, the salvation of infants also rests on it, not on baptism.

At what age have Baptists baptized? The emphasis of seventeenth century Baptist literature is on repentance from sin and faith toward God, both expressed voluntarily and publicly, as indispensable qualifications. Literature is silent about age. The Charleston Association's *A Summary of Church Discipline* (1733), influential in the South for a century, mentions no age but insists that "none is fit material of a gospel church without having first experienced an entire change of nature." The church's "door of admission" should not be opened "so wide as to permit unbelievers, unconverted, and graceless persons to crowd into it without control." To qualify for membership one must have some competent knowledge of divine and spiritual things. Subjects include sin, salvation through Christ, God's nature and works, Christ's person and works, the Spirit's works, and the important truths of the gospel and doctrines of grace.

Baptists have given little attention to setting a minimal age of admitting persons but much to defining qualifications of admission. Their practices have changed much, but their theory has changed little. Before 1875 the common practice was for a candidate to testify to his experience before the congregation. Church records repeatedly use the phrase "experience and baptism" in explaining the admission of new converts. Before 1900, however, the pattern was changing, largely under the influence of periodic revivalism. Churches gained numerous members during revivals or "protracted meetings." The large number of converts made it impracticable for the church to require a personal testimony of each convert. Since 1900, Baptists have tended to accept a public response to an invitation as symbolic of personal experience and to require no personal declaration before the congregation.

The age of baptism has dropped among Baptists. For two centuries most were baptized in upper teen-age or adult life. Using church and census records, I ascertained that a mid-Missouri Baptist Church baptized few persons younger than fifteen and none under twelve between 1820 and 1850. The age has steadily dropped in the twentieth century. Present-day Baptists blend education with revivalism as the technique of gaining converts. Through Sunday Schools they enlist prospects for instruction; through revivals they secure decisions among persons enlisted in the church's educational program. The median age of decision and baptism is probably ten to twelve at present, and it continues to drop. According to recent statistics, one out of two persons baptized in Southern Baptist Churches is twelve years or under, and one out of ten is eight or under.

At no time have Baptists required completion of a prescribed course of instruction as a prerequisite to baptism and church membership. They used catechisms until around 1900 but did not regard factual knowledge as the basis of baptism. In the mid-twentieth century some Baptist pastors have conducted a class for new members, but there is no uniform pattern. Sometimes instruction precedes baptism; sometimes it follows.

Conclusion

There has been neither uniform theory nor uniform practice relating to admitting children into the church during the last nineteen centuries. For at least two centuries, it appears, the early church did not baptize children. By 400 the doctrine of original sin had come to justify infant baptism. The early church required persons to acquire a basic knowledge of Christian truth before baptism.

During the Middle Ages confirmation came to be a sacrament completing baptism and administered after a period of instruction to persons baptized as infants. Protestants retained infant baptism, with most explaining it as a covenant-sign like Old Testament circumcision. All Protestants denied that confirmation is a sacrament, and originally they refused to practice it. Within a generation, however, confirmation appeared among them.

Most Protestants who baptize infants now have a service, usually preceded by a period of instruction, for admitting children to communion. Among denominations practicing believer's baptism only, particularly in the United States, the tendency has been to baptize candidates at an increasingly younger age.

Baptists have insisted that a church should consist only of regenerate persons admitted by believer's baptism only. But they now admit children to communion and to voting privileges at a younger age than do most Protestant Paedobaptists.

6

The Age of Accountability
William Hendricks

Introduction and Definition of Terms

The term "age of accountability" is not a biblical expression. The closest biblical reference to express the idea of accountability might well be Romans 14:12—"So then every one of us shall give account of himself to God." It is important to note that the Bible word used for account in this passage is *logos*. It is that same word used by John 1:1 to describe Jesus as God's Word—his account, or expression of himself to man.

As Baptists and some other Christians have used the term, "age of accountability" means a time or period of life when one is aware enough of God to respond to him. This response is inevitably rejection of God on the part of all men (Rom. 3:23). The relationship of one who consciously rejects God is estrangement—awareness of sin and limitation. The problem of "the age accountability" is particularly significant to Baptists because (1) they stress the necessity of conversion before church membership (2) they formerly, in some instances, set arbitrary ages at which children were accountable; (3) and they are facing today the dilemmas posed by "child evangelism."

It is not possible to answer the question, "What is the age of accountability?" until other, related questions are seen. These questions are: In what sense are all men responsible to God? What about the group and the individual in biblical teaching? How have succeeding ages brought changes from Bible times? What does the Bible specifically teach about the religious status of children? What are the minimal requirements for belief in God? We must also survey our contemporary Baptist practices in child evangelism and evaluate them carefully. These considerations will compose the bulk of this chapter. At the conclusion guidelines and suggestions will be made about dealing with children and assessing the "age of accountability."

In What Sense Are All Men Responsible to God?

Children are for real. They are people. C. S. Lewis in his remarkable books, *The Chronicles of Narnia,* has the white witch ask a child: "Are you human?" The answer, of course, is yes. Since children participate in humanness, in what sense are they responsible? The larger question should be approached first. In what way are all men responsible to God?

Genesis 1:26 indicates that man was made in the image of God. In Christian history there have been many diverse views as to what "image of God" implies. To this author the image of God means that man is capable of response to God. This response may be acceptance or rejection. The ability to respond to God is dependent on God's revelation of himself and God's help for every individual who responds to him positively.

The revelation of God to man is most clearly seen in Jesus Christ. Revelation comes into our world in Jesus Christ. The world, as we now experience it, exists in a lower key than God created it. We speak of this as "the fall." Sin as pride, rebellion, and desire are characteristics of all men. As pride, sin manifests itself primarily in man's refusal to accept God as God. Pride causes man to rely wholly on his accomplishments and to measure all things by his own discernment. Rebellion is manifested in rejecting the claim of God for ultimate allegiance to himself. Rebellion is more than the infraction of rules. It goes against the grain of what human nature itself really ought to be. Sin as desire is characterized by drawing all things into oneself for selfish purposes.

In these dimensions sin affects the entire structure of man's existence. Man raises himself to ultimacy—pride. He resists the just and ultimate claim of God on his life—rebellion. And he distorts all relationships of life by seeking them for selfish purposes—desire. It is to a world, less than ideal, and to men, distorted by sin, that the revelation comes.

Since the clearest revelation of God is Christ, man is fully responsible when confronted by Christ. Since responsibility is obtained in using the ability to respond, the actions of a man facing Christ and deliberately relating to him or refusing to relate to him brings the full status or responsibility. The Gospel of John states expressly that one is accepted or rejected by his belief or unbelief "on the Son" (16:8-11). It is furthermore stated that Jesus is "the way, the truth, and the life" (14:6). The clearest expression of the Christian faith is that men face God in the claims of Jesus Christ. In this confrontation full responsibility is attained.

But this clear expression is hedged in by pressing questions. Do men see God only in Christ? What of those who are never confronted by Christ in the proclamation of the gospel? When are children confronted by Christ?

Do Men see God only in Christ?—Christ expresses the fulness of what God is and what God desires to do for men. However, there is within man himself a "desire for God." This void in man is a preliminary preparation for the confrontation of God in Christ. This inherent religious bent is man's destiny. It is the crater or void which God fills with his love. Ironically enough, man seeks to fill this void of life with other things. This is tragic, because only God can fill that place.

In addition to the religious void in man's life, there is an awareness of both the grandeur and wretchedness of the world, that things are both greater than man could invent and worse than he can endure. This awareness points man to God; but again, only in a preliminary way.

It must also be seen that the line of special events in Israel leading up to the coming of Christ has much to say about God. The record of these events is the Old Testament. The Christian faith must retain the Old Testament because: (1) it acknowledges that he who created the world is involved in redeeming it; (2) it asserts that he selects certain men and events to express his wider purpose; (3) it claims the promise of a fuller and complete revelation of God is yet to come. In relation to this faith men of Old Testament times were redemptively related to God by faith in hope.

What of those who are never confronted by Christ in the proclamation of the gospel?—Full redemptive relation with God is unknown outside of Christ. This is the scandalously particular claim of the Christian faith (cf. Matt. 11:27). Men who are unconfronted by Christ find no adequate fulfilment of life's religious void. They likewise make wrong conclusions about what the world means and what life and destiny are about. They relate to God negatively by giving only human answers to the complexities of man and his destiny. This is a "lost" kind of existence. If they should learn of Christ and reject him, they are brought to full responsibility and full condemnation. This is the danger inherent in the Christian mission enterprise.

Christian teaching and compassion is motivated toward those who have not heard by three insights: (1) It is the specific intention of God that those who know him in Christ are under obligation to share him (cf. Matt. 28:19-20). (2) Judgment, or final status in life—here and hereafter—has degrees. Tyre and Sidon will be better off, in the last analysis, than the Pharisees who faced Christ and rejected him (cf. Matt. 11:22 and parallels). (3) Ultimately the fate of all men is in the hand of God, whose wisdom and justice is greater than that of men (cf. Isa. 40; Job 38-41; Rom. 14:12; John 5:22; 1 Cor. 1:18).

When are children confronted by Christ?—Full answers to this question can be given only after the larger considerations of this chapter have been explored. At this point several suggestions may be given: (1) Children are confronted by Christ when they receive Christly actions and attitudes from those about them. (2) Children are likewise confronted with Christ when they are taught and nurtured by the proclamation of the gospel of Christ. (3) They are confronted by Christ when the values and shape of their environment are formed by Christian insight. However, these confrontations are preliminary and preparatory. In the sense of full responsibility Christ confronts any individual in the proclamation of the gospel, by the power of the Spirit, at the time when the individual is aware of the message and meaning of the Christian gospel.

Two Biblical Insights

Biblical faith is always related to the individual and to the community of faith. These emphases form two poles of God's ways with men. In the Bible both are emphasized. For example, Moses, the psalmist, and Paul are illustrative of God's concern for the individual. The covenant agreement with Abraham and Israel, the corporate concern for the kingdom, and the New Testament concept of the church as Christ's body are illustrative of God's way of using the community of faith as an instrument of service and a witness of grace.

The individual and the corporate are well illustrated by the biblical expressions about Adam. Adam is an individual man, but he also is inevitably a picture of all men. His transgression is his; it was first. At the same time, it is a picture of what all men do. In him, as typical of what all do, men die and sin. All men do crystalize their own rebellion against God. No one is good when he is judged by what he ought to be. The Christian affirms that what man ought to be is seen truly only in Christ.

One of the most persistent errors about original sin has been the attempt to establish how we and Adam are connected. Historical theories of original sin have run the gamut. Some suppose sin is passed on by heredity like the color of the eyes. Others indicate that children have an inherent bent to sin.

Still others decry any liability to a child from his forebears. In this view men are neutral until they decide yes or no, pro or con.

These kinds of theories are intriguing, but they do not rise from the Bible so much as from our curiosity. The biblical view expresses the life of man as it exists. Individually men differ—yet, as a group and as individuals, they share a common lot. Man is sinful because he chooses to be. Two things are certain in the biblical picture of man: (1) He inevitably does sin. (2) He, as an individual in sin, must respond to God's grace in Christ for full redemptive relationship. The Bible simply does not say ultimately why man is a sinner. It does state unrelentingly that he is a sinner.

In ancient Israel it was felt that children were covered by the covenant of God within the elected community. This meant that individual children were considered under the protection of God until, by personal rebellion, they failed to obey him or refused to become a son of the covenant.

Evangelical Christians of the modern world share unusual and sometimes unwarranted anxiety about their young children and their status as individuals. This will be explored more fully in the next section. Ancient Israel assumed a covenant mercy of God to apply to their children. Jesus indicated his love for children and used their implicit trust as a model for what is required in biblical faith (Matt. 18:2-6). It would be unwise for us to become unduly anxious about the individual young child. We could do this to such an extent that we would not see him as part of humanity which is not yet capable of coping with grace.

We must keep the biblical balance of the individual and the corporate. Each child is born into a sinful humanity. All individuals eventually confirm themselves as sinners. It is God's purpose to save all. It is his manner to relate to humanity individually. This twofold biblical insight must be maintained. It must be maintained before conversion. We might say children are sinful because of their humanness but sinners because of their own choice. We must also maintain a perspective of the individual and the group at the time of conversion and after. One meets God individually because of the witness of the gospel borne by the community of faith—the church. The community proclaims the witness and the individual bears his witness in this larger framework. This is an indispensable insight to biblical thought. To place the individual in isolation from his common lot with humanity or from his place in the community of faith is not biblical.

The Shape of Things Since Bible Days

It is impossible to get "back to the Bible" without taking some of our own current concerns and interests with us. All men wear the glasses of their day and the outlook of their time. Several developments have risen since Bible days which complicate our view of children and their religious experience and expression.

Humanism.—Humanism arose in western Europe in the seventeenth and eighteenth centuries. Humanism is a way of looking at life which says that man is the measure of all things. There are certain similarities between humanist beliefs and the Christian faith. Both emphasize the individual. Both place high value on man and his abilities. However, the differences between humanism and traditional Christian belief are more pronounced than the similarities. Christianity sees man as the crown of creation but not as the measure of all things. The Christian view of man assesses his worth, but is also very aware of his weaknesses. For the humanist, man himself is the reference point for all value. For the Christian, God is the reference point for value.

Modern Western man is very much influenced, formally and informally, by the idea that man is the measure of all things. From this conviction have grown the modern sciences dealing with man and his distinctiveness: psychology, anthropology, sociology. Sometimes these studies and the ultimate concern with things human have so stressed the individual and his development that the corporate idea of humanity as a unit has been lost.

Psychology.—With the rise of modern psychology, the age of introspection began. Man has been studied from the view of the development of the self, the rise of his consciousness, and of the sources of his guilt. Complexes and neuroses are diagnosed and dissipated by those competent in helping man understand himself. Modern churches and parents reflect these insights when viewing their children's development. This is not necessarily wrong. However, caution must be taken lest we forget the broader biblical concerns of the whole of mankind, man's relation to the rest of creation, and man's obligation to God. Christians feel man's deepest obligations come objectively from outside a man—from God. They are not merely the product of man's inner reflections of guilt or anxiety.

More rapid maturation of children.—In recent times we hear of "the technological revolution" and the "knowledge explosion." Accelerated methods of transmitting vast amounts of factual materials are being perfected in education. Machines designed to teach and entertain are opening the universe and human nature before the eyes of children. One need look no further than the television set to find a reason today's youngsters are better informed about life at an earlier age than ever before.

Churches have been wise in using these perfected educational methods and devices. Children *are* maturing at a younger age today then formerly. Tests of children's alertness and ability are illustrating that children mature at different ages and according to their individual capacity. This fact does away with all attempts to establish a given and fixed chronological age as the time of accountability.

However, some problems also arise from this technological maturation. Are religious value and understanding given adequate exposure? Does the child see enough "value-building" programing on television? Are we forcing guilt on the young which is a guilt born from breaking the rules of our particular society rather than actually rejecting God in Christ? Are the "sins" children confess born of their despair in estrangement from God or are they born from the fear of displeasing those who demand a certain culturally conditioned way of life?

The above developments have all risen since biblical days. This does not mean that these concerns are not correct. Nor is it to imply that they do not have merit. However, it must be admitted, for example, that the meticulous searching of the "conscience" of a very young child has no biblical precedent. An abiding biblical insight is that God speaks to man at man's own level and in terms of a given man's own time. However, there is a core of belief which is essential to salvation in any age. The New Testament itself gives indication of this.

Requirements for Biblical Faith

Legalism is an abiding danger to biblical faith. The Pharisees of the New Testament evidence this. An equal danger to biblical faith is uncertainty or lack of belief. It is impossible to have saving faith in the fullest sense without certain minimal beliefs and awareness of those definitive acts which brought Christianity into being. Faith implies confidence in the object of faith. For Christians this means trusting God. Faith includes: the depth-level giving of oneself to God —the *heart;* the full willingness to pattern one's life according to the will of God—the *hands;* and a knowledge of who God is, what he has done for us, and what he requires of us—the *head.*

In the New Testament there is a basic, simple message (*kerygma* —the proclaimed truth). It was first delivered when the Holy Spirit came to complete God's revelation of himself and honor the work of Christ. Acts 2:14-36; 3:12-26; 4:8-12; 5:30-32; 10:36-43 contain, in embryo, what the remainder of the New Testament clarifies.

The basic points of the message of the early church are as follows: (1) Jesus came from God, the God of Israel who made heaven and earth. (2) Men killed Christ. The idea is later broadened to assert that all men and man as a unit in his sinfulness is responsible for Christ's death. (3) Yet, Christ's death was according to God's plan. That is, God was acting through Christ's death to bring man to himself. (4) Christ is raised. God in Christ has conquered even man's last enemy, death. (5) God through Christ has sent the Holy Spirit to bear witness to what God in Christ has done for man.

Without these facts the Christian faith is unintelligible. In these simple facts lies profundity which none has fully explained. This basic Christian gospel has been expanded; even in the New Testament itself further interpretation is given. This author feels that the message (*kerygma*) outlined in the early chapters of Acts may not be reduced. In other words, this is the heart of the Christian gospel. Men—all men—children as well, must have some awareness as to what this basic Christian message means to man.

In addition to hearing and affirming these facts man must do one other thing in salvation. That is, he must have faith—faith in the God who brought these things to pass. This faith in God is accompanied by despair of oneself and all other created things. This despair is evidenced by repentance. Repentance involves sorrow for sin. It is sorrow for having trusted in oneself, for having rejected God as alone worthy of our confidence, and for having sought all things for our own gain and desires. Contrast this notion of repentance for sin with the above threefold definition of sin.

I must be asked whether a child can understand, believe, and accept these things. This of course depends. It depends upon the child, his ability, his age, his capacity to grasp thoughts and make decisions. It depends on the language used to express these ideas and the illustrations used to clarify them. It depends on the family in which the child is reared and the interest of the parents in his education in things religious. Does a ten-year-old child understand and conceptualize these acts of God as he might at twenty or thirty? The answer is no. Can a child express the Christian gospel in adult terms and experiences? Again, the answer is no.

A further question should be explored: Are there perhaps two ways of relating to God, one for children and one for adults? Here we must give an emphatic no. An ancient heresy, gnosticism, taught that there were two types of salvation—one for those who were given holy knowledge (*gnosis*) and one for common men. It is perennially the temptation of the learned to ask that too much be believed.

The converse mistake is for men of good faith to suggest that one doesn't "have to believe anything to be saved." Trust God, it is enough! But what is trust, who is God, what has he done that man should trust him? Even the simple expression trust God or love Jesus implies some understanding. It is a Christian presupposition that no man can "understand" the Christian faith except that God by his Spirit aids him to do so. It is also a way of God with man that God aids man to the extent of man's ability.

Therefore, the matter returns once again to what God requires. He requires the proclamation of the gospel and its acceptance by man, by any man whom he enables to trust. The requirement is not less for children; there is only one essential gospel. The age of accountability must be related to the ability to grasp and accept the basic truths of the gospel.

What the Bible Says About Children

Children are for real. They are people, even if people in the minia-ture. If there is but one way to God, they too will come by the mes-sage of Christ. It is instructive, and somewhat surprising to discover exactly what the Bible says about children. Most of the biblical refer-ences to children are descriptive of some particular child. References are found to the child Moses, Ishmael, David's son who died in in-fancy, and Samuel. There are children in the Gospels, largely un-named, whom Jesus calls attention to for purpose of teaching and in illustrating his own compassion. A few general instructions about the training of children are found in the Old Testament wisdom litera-ture. References to Jesus as a child are present in the Scriptures, but there are not many.

An interpretation of biblical references to children would reveal the following conclusions. The childhood of important biblical figures is noted. Instruction of children by precept and example is com-manded. There is a great compassion for the young displayed in bibli-cal literature. As a whole, Bible references to children are descriptive rather than theological.

Questions We Should Ask

In the light of these larger questions there are many practices among Southern Baptists we need to explore more fully and evaluate carefully. Baptists have historically insisted on believer's baptism and regenerate church membership. Baptists today, in some ways, are more sensitive to the needs and capacities of children than were our forefathers at the turn of the century. We are definitely lowering the age at which children are baptized.

In 1966 there were 1,146 children five years of age and under bap-tized in Southern Baptist churches. In that same year we baptized 34,026 children ages six to eight, 139,211 children ages nine to twelve, and 59,569 children ages thirteen to sixteen (*The Quarterly Review*, Oct., 1967). However, it must be asked if there is not seri-ous tension between our historic principle of believer's baptism and our radical lowering of the age of those baptized? In the light of the above discussion there are other probing questions we should ask.

Are we holding our children responsible to God beyond their ca-pacity of belief and before the age of life commitment is possible? It is entirely possible that many expect the adult religious expressions and technical terms of the Christian faith to be meaningful to children. A young child would have much difficulty in comprehending words like: propitiation, atonement, repentance, or even faith. Full comprehension of these terms is often never reached by adults. Careful explanation and clear illustration should be given our children to aid them in grasping the "vocabulary of faith."

It may well be asked if a life kind of commitment to God can be made by children who are not accustomed to making significant and lasting decisions of any sort. Much of our theological anxiety about very young children is a projection of our own concern for them. There is no biblical reason one should not trust the compassion and mercy of God to extend to children until they can make meaningful and depth-level decisions for themselves. In fact the covenant of grace between God and mankind expressed in Christ, gives us every reason to presume that the young are kept by God in his compassionate concern.

The shape of things arising since Bible days poses other serious questions for us. Do we heighten the guilt of a child by our serious disapproval or rejection of him before he is able to comprehend why we feel he is wrong? Often parents commit serious errors by equating their cultural and social desires and values with the will of God. It is neither good procedure nor good theology to tell children God will not love them if they do thus and so. Is not the heart of the gospel God's love for sinners? Often we leave confused and uncertain minds by giving contradictory views of God. It is unfortunate some teach children only of God's goodness and love. When these children become a bit older, God is immediately portrayed as wrathful and angry. This is quite a confusing change in one week's time—the week of promotion. What is needed is accurate and balanced presentations of God to all age levels in our churches.

If the minimal requirements of faith are the basic demands of the gospel, are we insuring that those who express faith in Christ Jesus are aware of these requirements? In some way any regenerate person must be able to express and to relate them in a meaningful way to such notions as: who Jesus is; what he has done on our behalf; that his death for men is followed by resurrection; that God's Spirit honors the work of the Son in drawing men to God.

We must ask if our concern for children will permit us to have two ways of salvation, one for adults and one for children. Is it not possible we will price salvation so cheap that it will neither change our children nor sustain them through the troubled days of adolescence?

These questions and like concerns must occupy Southern Baptists as we look at the demands of biblical faith and the rising percent of our members who are unrelated to local congregations where they live.

Some Tentative Guidelines

To these complex problems there are no simple answers. However, some suggestions of a very practical nature may be steps in the right direction.

We must place more emphasis on a serious view of accountability than on the concept of age.—In the light of the demands of biblical faith we must present the one gospel as simply as possible. However, we must not reduce the full biblical expression of what is needed in salvation. It is highly doubtful that many children below the age of nine can express or have experienced despair for sin as radical separation from God. One cannot be "saved" until he is aware he is "lost."

It is a mistake to set an arbitrary age for conversion. It is likewise a mistake to ignore the capacity of given age levels.—Children do mature at different ages according to ability and background. God's Spirit does work with the individual in conversion. These considerations make it impossible to set any arbitrary age of accountability. Likewise, studies of age groups and their experiences show that abstract concepts cannot be grasped before a certain level of understanding is attained. It is also one of God's ways with man that he does not remove a person from his circumstances and ability in his work of grace. Both age and accountability must be considered. This is our perennial dilemma. We should seek to be more responsible in every way toward our proclamation of the gospel and in our guiding children toward conversion.

However, it must be stressed that if we continue to "invade the Preschool and Children's departments" for evangelistic prospects we are risking serious problems for the future. In doing this, we are also moving away from an adequate perspective of believer's baptism.

Better and more intensive counseling programs should be provided for children.—Conversion experiences, like all of God's ways with men, are highly individualistic. We must nurture children more carefully in their experiences of grace. There are incipient expressions of sin which are signs of a growing awareness of estrangement from God. We must not force these first feelers of conviction into a traumatic crisis for which the child is unprepared. In other words, children learn most things gradually by experience and over an extended length of time. The moment of guilt, acceptance, and conversion is some specific moment. However, to attempt to force that moment by confronting a child with an experience he has not had and a full un-understanding of the gospel which he cannot comprehend is disastrous.

It is disastrous because of later doubts he will have about the reality of his conversion. It is disastrous because many parents and churches will consider him "safe" and press on to other "prospects," leaving the child without further guidance or exploration of his experiences. It is particularly disastrous because this kind of pressure often disallows the indispensable role of the Holy Spirit in the conversion experience. More time spent with each child in preparation, conversion, and Christian growth is one effective means to correcting our noninvolved membership in Baptist churches.

Baptists must stress a theological awareness of the covenant mercy of God toward children to help allay the extraordinary concern of parents of very young children.—In many cases parents of very young children become anxious beyond the reason of biblical teaching for their children's salvation. In turn, they convey this anxiety to their children, who, eager to please, respond to what is expected regardless of the child's own comprehension. Baptist pastors are put under enormous pressure by some parents to insure the spiritual birth of their children. How is a pastor to respond to a parent who says: "I live with Johnny and know him well. I know he is ready for salvation, but I wish you would have a little talk with him"?

Such "little talks" are often less than ten minutes in duration. If a pastor is hesitant about the child's experience, many parents are outraged. If a pastor confirms this experience, it is taken as an external assurance for the parents' own feelings. Baptist pastors should preach specifically about children, their status before God, and what is the minimum requirement for salvation. If both child and parent hear these particular issues discussed from the pulpit and the biblical basis for all conversion taught carefully, they will have better grounds for making decisions.

We must have dialogue among pastors, evangelists, children's workers, and theologians.—In every walk of life there is a tension between the ideal and the practical, the theoretical and the actual. This is no less true among Baptist leaders who work with children. The deep emotional problems of adolescents about their religious experience are forcing Southern Baptists to explore what it means to be saved and to evaluate the age levels and experiences of those converted in early childhood.

It would prove very helpful to have statistics showing ages of conversion of those now active in Baptist churches. What percent of early experiences were followed by serious doubts and subsequent conversion experiences? This is not to suggest we should change the biblical norms because of our experiences. In reality all such changes should move in the other direction.

One thing we can and should do is to explore the idea of "age of accountability" with concerned and experienced people. Pastors, evangelists, children's workers, and Baptist theologians need to talk together candidly and with mutual appreciation concerning this problem.

Conclusion

The idea "age of accountability" has no definitive, biblical answer because it is not specifically a biblical question. Biblical materials do provide norms for what is required in salvation. A wise course is to correct our practices which do not preserve the full biblical meaning of salvation. The time of accountability is the moment of grace when one is brought to a decision for or against Christ by the Spirit. This moment requires the proclamation of the Word, the drawing of the Spirit, and the yielding of the individual to God. Until this moment is possible, one may leave children in the hands of God. Evidences are that we are holding very young children accountable for too much and not holding adults, who have professed Christ, accountable for enough.

7

Moral and Religious Growth
E. Paul Torrance

Religious educators in almost every major denomination are showing increased interest in scientific information about moral and religious growth and understanding among children. They frequently disagree about its relevance for religious education, but more and more such information is having an influence upon church programs for children.[1]

Some religious educators think that this kind of information is highly relevant to all problems in religious education for children. Koppe, writing in *Religious Education* in 1961, maintains that teaching techniques are effective only when they are consistent with the characteristic way in which children learn. He has suggested the following requirements for a developmental theory of moral and religious education:

1. It must be consistent with personality development.

2. It must be easily translated into program elements and teaching approaches.

3. It must describe meaningful developmental sequences of religious and character growth.

4. It must be applicable to all manner of men.

[1] I am greatly indebted to Dr. Ronald J. Goldman, head, Didsbury College of Education, Manchester, England, for many of the ideas contained in this paper. I have borrowed liberally from a study paper coauthored by Goldman and me.

5. It must take into account the dynamic nature of personality.

6. A meaningful theory of character development must be based on objective facts.

An equally deep respect for the child's natural way of development is reflected in the prolific work of Sophia Lyon Fahs. Her biographer summarizes Mrs. Fahs' attitude as follows: "Trust the child. Honor his integrity as an individual. In all his relationships expect him to grow as he grows; recognize the process as religious. Make it necessary for him to be resourceful and independent. . . . Teach him to be open-minded and yet not to be as 'a reed shaken by the wind.' Finally, have fellowship with him in experiences of appreciation of the wonder and the beauty and sacredness of life."

In opposition to the above attitudes, many religious educators still insist upon practices contrary to what is known about human development. They favor teaching the Bible and Bible stories to young children without considering whether they can understand the real meaning. They argue that we can enable children to grasp the message in nonverbal or relational ways. Some of them push for religious conversion and commitment even with four- and five-year-old children, but most of them admit that childhood is not the time for this.

Childhood is the time to establish a foundation of meaning upon which commitment can be built. Otherwise, when children grow up, they will reject our faith because they do not really know it or will settle for some hazy idea of Jesus Christ which is little more than superstition and almost totally lacking in power.

Religious educators who insist upon pressing for conversion, baptism, and commitment are ignoring some things about growth and development. Psychologists throughout the world have continued to find that the young child is not capable of abstract reasoning and cannot accept a philosophy of life. If pressed, such religious educators would have to admit that, according to their approach, learning is not closely related to experience. Conversion, they must assume, can precede a consciousness of sin, for the child is called upon to act on knowledge beyond his experience.

There are contrasting concepts of the purpose of religious education. Some workers see religious education as giving guidance to individuals and groups in a process of creative growth in the direction of mature religious concepts and behavior. Others emphasize the transmission of the Christian heritage, while a third group's major concern is with conversion and baptism.

In this chapter, I shall assume that all groups of religious educators have intellectual, emotional, and behavioral aims. Accordingly, I shall review some of the things educational psychologists know about growth in each of these areas and some of the major systematic attempts to examine moral and religious growth in each of these three areas.

Intellectual Growth

Information about the nature of intellectual abilities, intellectual functioning, and intellectual growth have expanded greatly during the last generation. The careful and rigorous work of psychologists has revealed a much more complex and diverse view of man's intellectual abilities than was held previously. The representation of human intelligence by means of an intelligence quotient (IQ) now seems primitive indeed and an insult to one of an infinite God's finest creations. The human mind and its functioning are infinitely complex.

There likewise has been a questioning of the assumption that abilities are fixed. In the past, the IQ was regarded not only as an estimate of total mental ability but was also looked upon as fixed and unchanging. Investigations have now cut to the root of these false assumptions with evidence that is indeed difficult to ignore or deny. The work of Jean Piaget, for example, provides a workable and more flexible alternative to the assumption of fixed ability since intelligence is conceived in an operational and dynamic sense.

Three stages of development are supported by a great deal of evidence in many areas of thinking. These stages, however, describe a continuous process of development in which each stage entails a repetition of processes of the previous level in a different organization. On the basis of his systematic study of children's religious thinking, Goldman expanded Piaget's three stages as follows:

(1) *Preoperational.*—Thinking goes from one particular to another particular and is limited by the particular state of the situation considered. The child centers upon one feature of a situation only and is unable to see relationships. He deals with only one problem at a time and cannot relate one problem to another in the same situation.

Thinking is unsystematic, fragmented, and inconsistent. The child cannot work back from an inconsistency.

(2) *Intermediate between preoperational and concrete operational.* —The child employs faulty logic and attempts to classify facts but breaks down. He considers more than one feature of a situation and attempts unsuccessfully to relate different facts. He is uncertain in his judgments. He attempts a crude and faulty kind of systematic thinking and his efforts to work back from an inconsistency usually end in confusion.

(3) *Concrete operational thinking.*—Logical thinking is limited to concrete situations, visual and sensory data. The child successfully classifies information and can relate two or more facts, but cannot generalize from one concrete field to another. He can work back from an inconsistency and concentrates upon relating things visibly or tangibly present. He tends to judge purely verbal problems in terms of their content and usually in terms of his own feelings and experiences.

(4) *Intermediate between concrete and formal operational.*—The child thinks at a more abstract level but is limited by concrete elements in the situation. His attempts at abstract and propositional thinking are not very successful. He tends to go outside of known information to form hypotheses but he is not very successful.

(5) *Formal operational thinking.*—The child is now able to engage in hypothetical thinking. He can now see information in terms of propositions, which are true or false and can be tested. He can think logically in symbolic and abstract form. He can see the incompatibility of certain facts with a hypothesis. He can start with a theory rather than with facts.

(6) *Advanced formal operations.*—The child can now state implications clearly and a higher level of formal or abstract thinking is evident. His hypotheses are much more ingenious than formerly but are realistic.

Goldman placed the preoperational stage at ages two through seven and maintained that children at this stage cannot understand Bible material at any rationally organized level. He placed the concrete operational stage at seven to eleven years and found that children during this stage are bound within concrete, materialistic, and literal interpretations of Bible truths. He found that it is not until the emergence of the formal operational stage at about age twelve that the child begins to develop a coherent intellectual picture of religious understandings.

Religious thinking is apparently not some special or separate mode of thought, but is a process of thinking identical with that exercised in other fields. Thus, moral and religious growth and understanding, like other aspects of development, are dependent upon varied sensory stimuli in the early years and upon a rich, stimulating, and responsive environment. Religious thinking is an attempt intellectually to relate and interpret these sensory experiences into a meaningful whole. Children will fail in this attempt at first, building up unrelated and inconsistent concepts. They must have a chance to explore and experiment with religious ideas, crude and alarming though these may appear to a mature, adult believer.

Generalizations have been made that before age four children approach religion in a disorganized and general sense; from four to seven years, they think in terms of fantasy; from seven until adolescence, their approach is factual, based upon the question, "Is it true?" and in adolescence they begin to explore the more searching and abstract questions about the nature of God and religion itself.

Language development is also relevant to the problem of moral and religious growth and understanding. Religious language must be seen as an informational system of sounds, which are accepted by children in the early years purely at the verbal level. Even the speaking religious vocabulary of young children is quite limited. Religious language is largely in terms of parables, symbols, analogies, inferences, and poetry. A literal acceptance of such language can lead only to gross confusion. Since its major purpose is lost, children seize upon nonessentials as important and frequently retard their insights.

The sustained use of religious language is meaningful only when the original experiences upon which the analogy, symbol, or parable is based, are known and to some extent understood. For example, "The Lord is my Shepherd" cannot be grasped beyond the visualized rote-memorized level until some experience of the helpless nature of sheep and the care of Palestinian shepherds is visualized. Only then can the inference and the analogy be recognized that as a Palestine shepherd is to his helpless, hungry, thirsty, fearful sheep, so is God to us.

This does not mean that we must wait until the child by chance learns about the nature of sheep before teaching the meaning of "The Lord is my Shepherd." Many things can be done to teach such a concept at an early age, but it requires the imaginative use of guided, planned learning experiences rather than just what the child happens to encounter.

Further analysis of religious language and its usage also reveals that its concrete imagery is essentially a vehicle for abstract thinking. Since at certain stages of development the child's thinking is self-centered, concrete, and materialistic, there are serious intellectual barriers. If asked to deal with a religious story before its truth can be recognized as the essential purpose of the story, the child's thinking may be crystalized prematurely at a concrete and material level and later insights may be difficult to achieve. A major problem then is to be aware of the child's level of development in providing religious experiences that will not handicap later understanding and acceptance of mature concepts.

Children are adept at using the language they are taught, as though they understood it. Teachers are often misled and attribute religious insights to them of which they are not capable. Frequently, they are incapable of making even the visual or auditory discriminations necessary to understand. For example, one mother noted that her four-year-old child was saying, "Howard be thy name," in repeating the Lord's Prayer. The pastor's name was Howard Giddens. It is doubtful that the child could discriminate the sounds in "Howard" and "hallowed." Certainly no one had explained to the child the meaning of "hallowed."

Thinking about time and space is also a process of mental growth and a variety of studies demonstrate that these skills are not available for understanding history and geography before the age of eleven or twelve years. An understanding of the Old Testament requires that a person grasp a historical sequence, set in a geographically complex area. Thus, these time and space concepts are basic to an understanding of the Old Testament and this makes us wonder how and when Old Testament teachings can be made intelligible to children.

In summary, it may be said that fixed ideas concerning the nature of intellectual abilities are giving way to a more dynamic concept in which the experience of the child is seen as an inescapably important element. The development of the thought processes involves the interaction between intellectual abilities and experience; concept formation is dependent upon rich stimulating experiences and a responsive environment. In the area of moral and religious development and understanding this stress upon experience is often observed in the form of a premature use of religious language and concepts not relative to the experience of children. At various stages, experiences may be explored through fantasy (drawing, dramatization, and stories) and only later intellectualized.

Studies of personality development reveal that emotions are dependent upon individual differences and experiences of the child from birth. All theories of personality draw attention to the importance of children's early experiences, and so do theories of moral growth. It is well known that even the infant responds to the adult's moral tone of voice and thus moral development begins. Many personality characteristics are modified or acquired by imitation of, suggestibility to, and identification with other persons.

In the early years, the dominant interpersonal relationships of the child are with his parents. As the ones who satisfy the basic appetites they are regarded as omnipotent. Feeding and elimination and those controlling these functions, primarily the mother, have a strong influence. In childhood, the relationships become more authoritative and the powerfulness of parents frequently gives way to figures of authority external to the family, such as teachers or ministers. Later, primary relationships move away from parents or parent symbols to peers, and social pressures from the peer group are felt and responded to and affect the growth of individual personality.

Many students of child development, among them Piaget, have called attention to the crucial period of disillusionment when he discovers that his parents are not perfect—that they do not always tell the truth, keep their promises, or practice what they teach. The sense of omnipotence and omniscience he felt his parents possessed is destroyed as the child observes them make mistakes of judgment or fact, become ill and even die, and be unaware when the child commits a forbidden act. In terms of religious development, this may mark the moment when the child turns from deifying his parents to "parentalizing" the deity.

Parents, however, still play decisive roles beyond this period in their children's moral and religious development. Studies of religious attitudes show with much clarity that attitudes of children and adolescents to religion almost invariably reflect the attitudes of their parents. There is also a highly significant correlation between attitudes of parents to religion and how children perform on tests of religious insight.

Peer group relationships exert considerable pressures, as shown both in the theoretical and experimental literature. In preadolescence and early adolescence these pressures appear to increase. The fact that children at these stages cannot bear to be different in dress, speech, and other matters from their peers may point to a particular danger in churches where there is great pressure for conversion in social groups. When it is the "thing to do," membership, conversion, or commitment may be embraced for this reason and not for reasons of personal conviction.

Sensitivity to relationships takes on newer dimensions after puberty with the development of heterosexual interests. The focus of emotionality upon sex is thought to mark the diminishing power to self-centeredness and the greater capacity to consider the needs of others. Sexual development also brings with it an awareness of certain taboos which arouse strong guilt feelings. These feelings, along with the conscious pursuit of love, make for tension and conflicting feelings. Out of these experiences, the young person can give himself to religion and receive experiences of cleansing and forgiveness. Phrases such as "giving yourself," "living a life of love," and "sacrifice for the love object" are common to adolescent emotionality and adolescent religious development.

Alongside this strongly positive potential motivation must be placed the objective and critical thinking common to this period of development. A desire to leave childhood behind may include an objection to religion as childish, if a literal interpretation of religion has not been previously transformed to a more spiritual interpretation. Investigators report that this tendency is quite strong among fifteen-year-olds, and that it is at about fifteen or sixteen that many people abandon formal religious allegiance because they equated it with childish thinking.

The subjects of these studies nevertheless voiced a strong desire to believe, a resentment that no alternative to "childish" religion was ever presented to them, and expressed an unsatisfied hunger to interpret life in spiritual terms. Together with the search for meaning, there seems to be a search for security, status, and significance. There is a sense in which all three are important to the growing child continuously through his development. There is also a sense in which each of them becomes a dominant concern in turn through childhood, early and later adolescence.

Differing needs are evoked at different times in development and differing goals are set by individuals to satisfy emotional needs. The role of experience is important and the most central experience is that of interpersonal relationships, first through parents, then through other children of the same age, and finally through heterosexual relationships. Religious development in these terms should be looked at in terms of a willingness to commit oneself to the Christian way of life and to accept and believe.

Acceptance and belief here should be defined in terms of the trust and love experienced in human relationships before they are directed to the person of God. It is a universal experience that no personal relationship is fully satisfying, and it is because the child becomes aware of this that one of the bases of religion is built. Too great a disillusionment with the most central relationship, that with parents, may create unhealthy needs that religion rarely satisfies.

Behavioral Growth

Behavior is an overt expression of information (intellectual development) and motivation (emotional development) and is largely learned. Already, we have noted how children are open to imitation, suggestion, and identification in their behavior. Even such a family factor as personal appearance may be partly learned, and facial expressions, habits of smiling, or physical posture may explain some family resemblances.

Parents, schools, churches, and the law exert pressures upon the child to behave in certain situations in specific ways. Social group pressures or those involved in heterosexual relationships enforce other kinds of behavior and an area of conflict often occurs when social group and parental demands differ. Children frequently become skilled in learning separate, specific, and sometimes opposing behavior patterns, adapting with ease to the expectations of those with whom they are concerned in a particular situation. Others experience great pain as a result of these conflicts.

Implicit in all behavior is a system of signals gradually developing into an organization of moral values. This may be generalized as a process of passing through sequences of prudential, parental, peer, and personal morality. What is regarded as right or wrong behavior is first dependent upon prudence (what is right is pleasurable and what is wrong is painful); upon parental authority (it is right because parents say so); upon peers (what is proved by the group is right); and personal conviction. These may be termed the moralities of fear, respect, social conformity, and personal conviction.

This sequence follows rather closely the findings of Piaget of the development of moral judgment. In the child's development of the idea of justice, Piaget found behaviors regarded as unjust, occurring developmentally somewhat as follows:

(1) *Behavior that goes against commands received from adults— lying, stealing, and breakage.*—We observe this in the guilt expressed even by a three- or four-year-old when he spills his milk at the dinner table, or in the six- or seven-year-old when he is so strongly tempted that he steals the money lying on the dresser.

(2) *Behavior against the rules of the game.*—A Little Leaguer can be quite vehement with another when he fails to observe a common rule such as keeping the correct distance in pitching.

(3) *Behavior against equality.*—Teen-agers are real crusaders for equal rights as we have seen in the early Negro demonstrations and the more recent demonstrations of the Latin-American "Brown Berets" in the Los Angeles area.

(4) *Acts of injustice connected with adult society.*—Today there is an increasing awareness throughout the United States of acts such as union discrimination, general animosity against Negroes and other minority groups, and the like. The developmental nature of these classifications is reflected in the following distributions of observed behaviors of six- to eight-year-olds and nine- to twelve-year-olds among the four categories listed above.

	Forbidden	Games	Inequality	Social Injustice
6-8 yrs.	64%	9%	27%	0%
9-12 yrs.	7%	9%	72%	11%

Piaget maintains that the main factor in the conformity of very young children to the commands of adults is nothing more than respect for age. Right is to obey the will of the adult; wrong is to have a will of one's own. For older children, right depends upon mutual agreement and there is greater moral solidarity with age.

Moral values are, of course, allied to religion, but in a broader sense the Augustinian concept of "Love God and do as you like" reveals the right relationship between religion and morality. In this context, if love is the basic expression of religion, specific rules and concrete commandments are unnecessary. Dominatingly negative rules are bound up with some expressions of the Christian faith, such as the "thou shalt not" commandments. Because such negative rules appear so much in their Sunday School literature and in the teaching and preaching of the church, children apparently associate Christianity with negative rules.

It is, of course, not the task of the psychologist to determine the "rightness" or "wrongness" of values. This is the task of religion. The psychologist's task is to determine under what conditions values are learned and what effect they have upon personality development, intellectual development, and behavior.

Religious behavior may be defined both in a narrow and a broad sense, namely the practice of religious habits of worship, prayer, meditation, and Bible study, and also the overt application of attitudes and values to personal relationships. Development here is extremely difficult to define, for there are differing levels of readiness during a child's development in the direction of mature behavior. There is a tension, a point of balance, between what is possible for a child to do and what is expected of him. The expectation itself will increase his capacity to respond, but if it is too high and too demanding it will result in moral failure and inhibitive guilt in the child.

The proper age for a declaration of faith or conversion and baptism has been of much concern in almost every religious group. The response that one makes to this issue must of course depend on his view of the nature of the declaration and its implications. It may also be determined by his interpretation of what is known about moral and religious growth and understanding. In a recent symposium, spokesmen for thirteen different religious groups discussed this problem in the light of the practices among their groups. There seems to be a general tendency for most of these religious educators to place the proper age for the major declaration of faith within their groups at about twelve years or shortly thereafter.

Denton Coker represented Southern Baptists and expressed the view that the making of an intelligent declaration of faith in Christ requires a degree of maturity in abstract thinking that is usually not found until adolescence. He also contended that to commit oneself to become a disciple of Christ necessitates a sense of personal independence, implies the embracing of a new way of life, and a readiness to participate responsibly in the life of the Christian fellowship.

In each case, Coker expressed the belief that such levels of development generally are not achieved until adolescence. He emphasized the point, however, that we should avoid specifying one point in a person's life before which he cannot make a serious declaration of faith in Jesus Christ, since such an act is a response to a divine-human encounter.

It can hardly be said, however, that all Southern Baptists share Coker's views on this issue. Many observers report that there has been a growing tendency among Southern Baptist churches for children to profess a religious conversion at a continuously earlier age and that it is not unusual for preschool children (four- and five-year-olds) to be accepted for church membership and baptized.

It is well known that the wide range of individual differences in development make such a question difficult to answer. The role of the Holy Spirit, however, makes this problem even more difficult. A psychological description of the work of the Holy Spirit can only describe it in terms of human behavior brought about by experiences that stimulate responses to the unusual or imaginative.

If we agree that religious experience is ordinary experience understood at full depth, then the moving of the Holy Spirit may be seen in the creative ways men respond to their everyday experiences. The evidence seems to indicate that genuinely creative responses are not achieved by logical means. Creatively derived solutions may of course be tested by the rules of logic and evidence, but this is not the way the solution, idea, or other response occurred in the first place.

As I have suggested in *Education and the Creative Potential,* religious development is not usually linked with creative behavior and creative ways of learning, but with authoritative teaching and acceptance. This, of course, is contrary to the way in which Jesus himself guided or provoked his followers to learn. He was a questioner, an arouser of curiosity in others, and provoked people to search into, to translate and rethink the stories he told. As a Hebrew youth, Jesus of course had doubtless had to memorize reams of Scripture, and there is certainly a place for memorization in modern religious education.

Jesus, however, did not stress the memorization of Scripture, but rather he made creative use of Scripture by stimulating people to understand it and bring fresh insight to it. He was more interested in sincere, insightful, creative, and personal responses than in insincere, authoritatively accepted, and uncreative ones.

The essential, fundamental, initiating phase of all creative behavior seems to be a sensitivity or openness to problems, difficulties, missing elements, and the like. This brings about a discomfort that motivates the further phases of the creative process. In terms of religious experience, this discomfort, disturbance, or upset may be the working of the Holy Spirit.

Children and adolescents frequently give evidence that they experience a discomfort and concern about problems but rarely are given opportunities to share and explore them because an authoritarian approach to truth discourages them. Rather than ignore questions or accept them grudgingly, religious education teachers should welcome, utilize, and help provoke them. Problems, both intellectual and emotional, may be avoided and covered up too easily and block the child's search for solutions.

What about creative functioning on the production of ideas for solutions? What about flexibility of approaches in thinking to meet changing conditions and in examining problems from different viewpoints? Originality—making mental leaps away from the obvious —and elaboration—working out of the details of a solution—have obvious relevance to religious behavior. The Holy Spirit may be regarded as a moving force in each process. If we accept the role of the Holy Spirit as the divine agent stimulating man to explore and integrate his experiences, the development of creative behavior becomes an important aspect of moral and religious growth and development.

Conclusion

In a brief review of this type, many important aspects of moral and religious growth and understanding must necessarily be left untouched. It is hoped, however, that this review has presented enough information to support the following generalizations:

1. Healthy moral and religious growth and understanding is consistent with general human development in all of its aspects—intellectual, emotional, and behavioral. This is in accordance with God's plan.

2. There is a time lag between firsthand experience of life and abil-

ity to understand religious language and concepts. A child must experience "love" before he can understand its meaning.

3. There is a danger that premature religious language and suggested or required religious responses too early can interfere with religious growth and understanding. Four- and five-year-old children who are required to sing, "We are little Christian children . . . Christ, the Son of God most dear, died upon the cross to save us," or, "God gives us all our pretty toys," is bound to find the experience confusing both now and later.

4. Emphasis should be placed upon feeling in those conditions or situations such as cooperative activities, creative dramatics, and service projects that will facilitate moral and religious growth and understanding.

5. There are many individual differences in moral and religious growth, as in all other kinds of human growth. No one should expect all children to develop morally and religiously at the same rate or according to the same pattern.

8

The Child and the Home
Clifford Ingle

In the delightful book *Come Home with Me*, Hannen Foss says: "There is no substitute for family life, and nothing can replace parental responsibility. If the home fails to make its designed contribution to the education of the child and his preparation for life, no [other] education plan can make it good. For that reason the restoration of the ideal of the Christian family, is among the foremost tasks of our time."

This quotation eloquently emphasizes a fundamental principle of this chapter, namely, any theology of children and the church must consider the relationship of parent-child in a family setting and give thought to what the church can do to strengthen this relationship. A church's concern for the Christian upbringing of children during the first years of life should be family oriented. Therefore, this chapter will emphasize the family and the early years of childhood. The discussion will be a development of four basic ideas: the importance of the home, family roles in a changing society, what constitutes a good home, and some practical suggestions.

The Importance of the Home

The home is the laboratory of life. It is the place where character is first developed, and the reality of God is first discovered.

The fields of psychology, sociology, psychiatry, educational research, and testing are providing an increasing volume of information concerning the priority of the home and its influence upon personality development. The following statements are typical of those being made by leaders in these areas: Ernest Ligon says, "The influence of the home upon the child is at least thirty times as strong as that of the church and the school. Without it, the church is helpless." Paul H. Vieth puts it, "The family is primary in God's economy. . . . Nowhere else may religion be taught so easily and with such abiding results as in the home." William H. Genné says, "In a society in which most organizations, including churches, are growing larger and less personal, the family remains the one stronghold of intimacy."

Many others could be cited, but two are sufficient. Abraham N. Franzblau writes, "Insights stemming from psychiatry, have emphasized . . . the parents as the most important teachers. It has also shifted to the early years of childhood our concept of what is the peak in the process of moulding character." Edith F. Hunter says, "Unless the churches become more concerned with and aware of the day-by-day religion that its member families are living, they will play an ineffectual and trivial role."

All statements, expressions, and actions concerning the importance of the home are brought to sharpest focus in Luke 1:30-31: "The angel said unto her, Fear not, Mary: for thou hast found favour with God. And, behold, thou shalt conceive in thy womb, and bring forth a son, and shalt call his name Jesus."

Family Roles in a Changing Society

The importance of the home should be viewed in the light of the rapid change of social structures in today's world. Dr. Marjorie Stith, head of the department of Family and Child Development, Kansas State University, gives six important influences which bear upon the role of the family in American society.

These are: (*1*) *A change in family composition.*—This is to be seen in such things as marriage at earlier ages, an increase in illegitimacy, and a greater number of incomplete families. (*2*)*An increasing span of human dependency as witnessed in the emphasis upon continuing education and the increase of life expectancy.*—The number of persons both under eighteen and over sixty-five increased almost twice as fast as the rest of the population. Consideration must be given to the financial assistance given by parents to their married-in-college children, retirement, and care for the aged.

(*3*) *Urbanization and industrialization.*—The present trend toward

great cities, automation, and technology brings about a massing together of people which tends to weaken the cohesive forces of family
living and to open possibilities for family disorganization. *(4) Poverty in the midst of affluence.*—While more than half of all American
families have an average income of over six thousand dollars, 20 percent (approximately 40,000,000) of our population live below the
poverty line. Chronic unemployment, which has resulted from a de-
creased need for unskilled labor, continues to create problems in family
living such as housing, food, health, education, and family planning.

(5) The role of women.—Women are seeking educational and em-
ployment opportunities and are planning careers along with marriage
and family relationships. More than half of the women who are em-
ployed are married. Three out of every ten mothers with children
under eighteen years of age are working outside the home. The freedom and choice of working is increasingly open to women. *(6)
Changing power structures and divisions of labor.*—Functions once
considered to be family responsibilities are now being carried on by
other institutions. There is less a division into what was considered to
be "man's work" and "woman's work." The loss of parental authority
has led to uncertainty in dealing with children which in turn makes it
difficult for youth to find adequate standards of responsibility and
conduct.

What shall we say and do concerning the role of the family in a
rapidly changing society? The pessimist will undoubtedly sigh for the
return of the "good old days," while solemnly affirming that contemporary family life is doomed to destruction. The optimist sees a
golden opportunity for an improvement of the human condition in
every area and on every level. Change *is* upon us! So the Christian
must consider the implications of change for the family and devote
careful thought to responsibilities and opportunities of the family and
the church in contemporary society.

Qualities Necessary for a Good Home

When is a home good, strong, and healthy? What does the
preacher mean when he talks about the necessity for a good home?
When is a home truly Christian? After some four to six years of
study, the research specialists at the Character Research Project,
Union College, published the following findings concerning qualities
(dimensions) which constitute a healthy, strong, and good home:

Qualities of the wife and mother: 1. She has the capacity to channel her emotions and those of her family into positive emotions, such as enthusiasm for life, love, faith, and general warmth of affection. Her husband and children do not have to be told of her love; they feel it as her very being is one of outgoing warmth and affection. She has faith in them, herself, and God.

2. Her discipline is through poise and selflessness. It is natural to her character. She does not fly into a rage or nervous tension. She does not give punishment for punishment's sake. Neither does she resort to self-pity as a means of bringing a sense of shame and guilt to the offenders.

3. She has acquired the skills of parenthood. She loves being a wife and mother. Her ideals are similar to the college student who, upon being asked concerning her goal in life, replied, "I can think of no other goal as high as being a good wife to the one God has for me and to be a good mother of our children." Skills of parenthood include also the ability of family worship, meeting social and emotional crises, and mastering the unexpected.

Qualities for the husband and father: 1. The first and strongest quality can be described as kindness, gentleness, and thoughtfulness, plus an invincible faith in his children. Such kindness and gentleness are not to be considered as synonymous with soft, namby-pamby wishy-washiness. Rather they are marks of genuine piety and manhood. Doubt fosters doubt. Suspicion arouses suspicion, but an invincible faith in his children creates in them the feeling of worth, importance, and confidence.

2. Dependability. He is a solid citizen who makes his family a contribution to the community. He takes an active interest in his children's activities and interests. They know they can count on him and feel secure in this knowledge.

3. The third quality is energy and enthusiasm. He is a man of action. The word "enthusiasm" comes from the Greek, meaning to be possessed or inspired by the gods. It means to be caught up in a cause, to be sold on one's subject, to be filled with vigor. It involves a deep feeling of eagerness to achieve. It arises out of a sincere faith. Religiously, it means that the man has deep religious convictions and that religion is a practical everyday affair.

Qualities for the home: 1. There must be the involvement in a positive way of the emotional energies of the members of the family.

Emotional energies are always present and can destroy the home or make it great. These energies may be channeled into negative emotions of anger, fear, worry, rage, depression, suspicion, or irritability. (What a tragedy it is for children and husband to be daily submitted to a whining, complaining mother who resorts to feigned illness and self-pity, or for the children and wife to be daily submitted to a hot-tempered, demanding, authoritative, pessimistic father.) In a good home the emotional energies of each member are channeled into such emotions as love, magnanimity, courage, enthusiasm, optimism, and faith.

2. The primary meaning of the word "discipline" is to teach or to instruct. From the New Testament viewpoint it means the process of teaching and training by which the person is increasingly formed into the image of Christ. Such discipline is borne out of genuine love and concern for one another. Therefore the attitude in which discipline is given is far more important than how strict or lenient the discipline may be. The child should get the overall feeling that discipline is for his benefit, not for the benefit of his parents. One child specialist has said that ultimately you can discipline only those children who make themselves your disciples.

3. Each member of the family has an important role. This involves the development of a feeling of personal worth and dignity. Each person feels that "what I do is important." Parents will be on guard in comparing the accomplishments of the children. For example, in one home where a younger child was reminded constantly of the outstanding attainments of the older child, he, in a burst of anger and desperation exclaimed, "Listen, I am me! Doesn't anyone know me?"

4. The home's positive contribution to the community means more than simply doing nothing that is offensive or living in isolation. No home is great whose members live only for themselves. It involves knowing one's neighbors, of sharing in community aims and projects. The members of the family become active participants in building a better community.

Some Practical Suggestions

An understanding of the importance of the home and qualities which constitute a good home is not enough. If the churches are to uphold the values of family life they must assist the family to function —as a family. Opportunities for the family to be together and grow together must be strengthened, not hindered. Most observers of religious education indicate that churches and denominations have either abandoned a relevant home ministry or usurped the prerogatives of the home into an institutional church. A religious survey of the literature of five major Protestant denominations bearing upon the general subject of parent-child relationships reveal:

(1) Too often there was the failure to take seriously the age level, capacities, abilities, needs, and the developmental processes of the child under two years of age. The "little adult" concept still dominates most religious literature. (2) Little if any attention was given to the importance of the child's emotional development, especially in relation to his mother and father. (3) Most of the literature was content oriented instead of process oriented. It was an intellectual approach concerned with ideas rather than concerned with capacities for relationships. (4) Some of the literature was of doubtful value because it was merely a duplication of secular writings and had little if any distinctive Christian significance.

The churches must search for an understanding of those forces which undergird the home and provide the necessary means of assisting these forces to function properly. The readers are referred also to chapter 12 of *Teaching for Results*, by Findley B. Edge for a good discussion of church-home cooperation. The *Home Life* magazine published by the Southern Baptist Sunday School Board is strongly recommended. It should be sent by the church into the homes of its members. Following are some suggestions which the writer believes to be vital to carrying out an adequate home ministry.

Preparation for marriage.—There is a sense in which a man and woman are preparing for parenthood during the years of childhood, adolescence, and maturity. Each person brings to marriage and parenthood only that which they are at that particular time. The kind of person their child will become is largely determined by the kind of persons the parents are, and by their relationships with each other. For the church or the parents to wait until the child is born to begin a spiritual ministry to him might be compared to making an effort to board an airplane that has already left the runway.

Church libraries should contain books dealing with the psychological characteristics of the various ages, sex, personal identity (who am I?), a Christian view of man and the universe, vocations and vocational choice, and preparation for marriage. The denomination should

provide attractive, inexpensive (or free) literature on such subjects as
"Choosing a Life's Mate," "A Christian View of Marriage," and
"How to Build a Christian Home." There might be great virtue in de-
voting an entire quarter of Sunday School lessons for children and
youth on preparing for marriage. Such a vital matter should be presented through the organization with the largest attendance. A series
of sermons on the general theme of "Youth Facing Life Today and
Tomorrow" would be more appropriate than a dozen sermons on
divorce or the military crisis.

Churches should provide counsel for those planning marriage.—
Strong language must be used here. Far too long have ministers delivered sermons full of "sound and fury" concerning the high divorce
rate and the disintegration of home life; yet they perform the wedding
ceremony for any who may come to their door. It is the contention of
the writer that ministers and churches must share in the guilt of the
deterioration of family life by not providing adequate counsel for
those contemplating marriage.

Dealing with a bewildered and lonely child whose parents are di-
vorced is exceedingly difficult. How much better it would have been
for the church to have begun early in providing necessary counsel, literature, and training in preparing individuals for family life, thus
giving a young couple more assurance of a durable and happy marriage. The book *To Understand Each Other* (Richmond, Va.: John
Knox Press), by the famous Christian psychiatrist, Paul Tournier, is
strongly recommended for those planning marriage as well as for
those who are married.

Dr. John Howell, professor of Christian Ethics, Midwestern Baptist Theological Seminary, has produced a guide which he uses in premarital counseling. In it he suggests five, forty-five-minute counseling
sessions. The content of the sessions is listed below and offered as a
guide to ministers and churches. The number and length of the counseling sessions is usually determined by the particular situation. The
subjects discussed are:

    I. Understanding marriage (first session)
      1. The Christian view of marriage
      2. The basic purpose of marriage
      3. The true nature of marriage
   II. Harmony in marriage (second session)
      1. Spiritual harmony

      2. Emotional harmony
      3. Physical harmony
  III. Making marriage a partnership (third session)
      1. A partnership in love
      2. A partnership in finances
      3. A partnership in recreation
      4. A partnership in worship
      5. A partnership in home building
  IV. Preparation for parenthood (fourth session)
      1. Planning for children
      2. Responsibilities for parenthood
      3. Some rewards of parenthood
   V. The wedding ceremony
      1. Some necessary considerations
      2. Significance of the ceremony
      3. Meaning of the vows
      4. After the ceremony

The purpose of premarital counseling goes beyond assisting a couple to get married. It also must make available all the resources of the church to the couple and their families as vital to their continuing life together. One of the most significant by-products of such counseling is a new relationship between the couple, pastor, and church. Few programs in the life of a pastor and church will pay such dividends as this type of counseling ministry for those planning marriage.

The husband and wife need spiritual instruction concerning the birth and care of children.—Birth is history past. It is the individual's first step toward gaining independence. However, even before entering the world, the baby is already a product of his relation to his mother. The way he will respond to his new environment has been influenced by his prenatal experience and mothers should know this. Recent studies have revealed that the unborn child may be influenced in a negative way by any or all of the following:

1. Maternal malnutrition
2. Drugs such as LSD. Also smoking.
3. Irradiation
4. Maternal diseases, such as German measles
5. Rh factor
6. The age of the mother

7. Maternal emotional states

8. Maternal attitudes (psychiatrists are saying that some miscarriages may be due to the unconscious rejection of motherhood on the mother's part).

The attitude of the husband during the days of his wife's pregnancy and the days immediately following is of utmost importance. Marriage counselors remind us that for most individuals, including other children, pregnancy and birth may be a time of family crisis which may lead to separation and divorce.

That it is equally important that the husband be prepared to understand and accept his role during the days of his wife's pregnancy and the days immediately following. Does he show real concern for his wife's emotional and physical condition, or does he use various means of seeking to isolate himself from that which he considers to be of little interest to him until the day of the "blessed event"? Does he become defensive and abusive in being "left out"? Does he point out his wife's faults?

A husband should know that his wife's emotional, mental, and physical condition is affected by his attitudes and actions. He is responsible for giving the proper love and attention to his wife as befitting one who takes seriously the fact that a child is created by an act of *two* persons, behind whom stands the holy God.

Both husband and wife should be led to see that all care of the newborn child should be loving care. No care in the form of giving things, no matter how efficient, can substitute for the outgoing love of parents.

Randolph Crump Miller of Yale emphasizes the importance of loving relationships by saying: "At the moment of creation personal relationships determine what will happen to him. . . . What parents are, makes the difference. They teach through *their relationships* with their children. They show what love means by the simple act of loving. They indicate the forgiving and redemptive love of God by their own capacity to restore their children to family fellowship . . . the parents provide the atmosphere in which children can grow . . . under direction and guidance."

Both parents must accept the responsibility for a new life. Other children will also have to face this phase of emotional change and readjustment. Therefore, relevant literature and classes providing instruction for parents-to-be are both realistic and practical. Bible study and worship simply cannot meet all the needs of persons facing parenthood.

Parents need assistance in understanding the growth processes of children and the role parents play in such growth.—There is available a vast literature on the subject of child growth—biologically, socially, intellectually, and spiritually. Therefore, the primary concern of this topic is to examine that phase of a child's experience which is basic to his growth, the relationship of love.

The infant is totally helpless. He is so ill-equipped to face the world that, if left alone even for a short time, he would perish. He is made to be cared for. He grows through loving relationships. The one thing he is equipped to do is to express his feelings by means of sound for relational experiences such as cuddling. Child specialists are quick and gesture. Such expressions are not only for organic needs but also to point out that such experiences as cuddling and other means of tender care are an absolute necessity for the infant, that he cannot exist in isolation.

The infant comes into the world as a bundle of emotions without a developed intellect. The basic motivations (emotion, drive, instinct) are love (trust, faith, security) and hate (fear, anger, distrust). These remain the basic aspects of all subsequent human motivation. In the infant love consists of the sense of comfort which is communicated through his expressions of satisfaction. Hate is present as the discomfort felt in a lack of organic needs or isolation.

For example, every infant needs the emotional satisfaction, love, and security which comes from being nursed and cuddled. Feeding the child when he is hungry is usually the most desirable practice. Prolonged hunger and crying while the mother faithfully adheres to a rigid schedule creates in the child states of tension which may initiate personality difficulties.

Dr. J. A. Hatfield, in *Childhood and Adolescence,* presents one of the best outlines of child development; and Dr. Lewis J. Sherrill, in *The Struggle of the Soul,* deals with the development of religious and moral concepts. Both books (paperbacks) are recommended to parents. Dr. Hatfield suggests that the first two years of life witness the emergence of biological instincts and potentialities necessary to survival. The third year through the fifth or sixth years are engaged in the organization and harmonization of these various impulses under the control of a developing will. He suggests that during the first five

or six years of life a child goes through the following stages of personality organization:

1. Total dependence upon the mother or mother substitute.

2. Imitation: This begins a few weeks after birth, and through it
the child takes over the actions and standards of others. If a parent
acts cruelly, the child will act cruelly; if the parent acts lovingly, the
child will act lovingly. Imitation is the basis of the learning process.

3. Suggestibility: Here the child takes to himself, not only the actions, but also the moods, feelings, and ideas of others. Usually it is a
subconscious process.

4. Identification: This is the natural outgrowth of suggestibility, as
here the child tries to take to himself the entire personality of the
other person or thing. He is no longer a little boy or girl; he is an en-
gine driver or she is a mother.

5. The personality formation of the ego ideal: Here the child dis-
cards the person or thing but keeps the character, which becomes a
part of his own personality. Instead of saying, "I am brave like
Daddy," he, having incorporated his father's standard says, "I am a
brave boy." He has now established within himself the guiding principles by which he can control and direct all native impulses, and so
harmonize his personality.

The majority of child specialists state that the foundations of personality are formed in the early years. If the child's personality is well
organized, if the impulses are fully expressed and usefully directed,
then the child will be strong in will, happy in disposition, and of good
character. However, if there is a failure in organization, the child may
be incapable of facing the responsibilities of life. This is the reason
why most psychopathologists believe the predisposing causes of neu-
rotic behavior disorders originate in the first few years of life. This
also points up most eloquently that a church dare not usurp the prerogatives of the home, nor the mother forsake the early care of her
children.

Long before the child can comprehend the meaning of religious
concepts, his experience with his mother or mother substitute is shap-
ing the kind of person he becomes and is laying the basis for his future religious experience.

The claim is being made that the emotional life of the infant determines the kind of religion to which he can respond and make his own.

Thus the interaction between parents and child in the first years of life has profound significance in laying the foundations of the child's religious development. The child is forming emotions, both love and hate, which develop into attitudes that will direct him either toward or away from God.

The possibility of trust in God, therefore, begins to be shaped by the child's first relationships with his parents or parent substitutes. In his first three or four years, religious words and concepts have little significance for the child. The basis of his reaction to those words and concepts is being formed by his relationships with his parents.

Instruction in content and religious practices belong to a later period of the child's development. In reality, what the child knows by the time he is five to seven years of age is almost trivial. What he has come to feel at that age may be life or death. It may not be vital that little children be *taught* the doctrines of the faith their parents and the church profess, for they can understand very little anyway.

It is imperative, however, that during infancy and early childhood they see and feel that there are mysteries which they cannot understand but which have deep meaning to their parents. In the fulness of time the desire to know and to participate in those mysteries will come. Then he will be teachable, and he will be inclined to follow. However, if he feels that these things make no real difference to his parents, his being forced to attend church and to learn details of the faith will contribute little to his religious development.

Churches need to provide an adequate ministry to those whose homes have been disrupted by death, separation, and divorce.—Such happenings usually leave children bewildered and lonely. In fact, a home broken by divorce is often more tragic than one broken by death, because the events and atmosphere preceding the divorce play havoc in the child's personality development. The denial of love, attempted explanations, remarks by friends, and facing society—all throw a burden upon the child and remaining parent which they should not have to bear. The child, as well as the separated parents, desperately needs the ministry of love, understanding, and acceptance which Christ has committed to his churches.

The churches must recognize the home as the child's first and major center of worship.—Not the church, the pastor, nor the teacher, but the parents are the first teachers of religion. That which goes on in the home has greater influence on the little child than that which happens in a church building on Sunday. Parents are the first persons who are directly responsible for the religious welfare of their children. The home is the center of worship. Anxious parents may ask, "But what can we do?" The following suggestions are offered as ways through which your home may truly be a center of worship:

1. Create a religious (worshipful) atmosphere. This does not mean "churchiness or playing church." Neither does it refer to negative attitudes or a rigid set of rules. Such matters are foreign to the teachings of the New Testament. Rather we mean that worship (awe and reverence before God) as a daily affair has a natural spontaneity of happiness and joy. Simple religious expressions, actions, and prayers; appropriate religious art and literature are excellent aids in creating the proper atmosphere so necessary to lift little children toward God. Parents need to know that living the presence of Christ is not to be an isolated event on Sunday; the daily life of expressing feelings and ideas in simple terms offers purpose and guidance to the child.

2. Worship opportunities. An atmosphere is created by specific attitudes and actions. Such attitudes and actions of worship should occur in the home so that the child grows, never recalling *the* first moment he learned about God. Worship opportunities are created as a natural part of living by such things as parents' humming or singing hymns, saying bedtime prayers, having a time of family devotions with all members present, and the religious observance of specific events. For children, a spontaneous burst of praise from a parent may accomplish more than long and monotonous prayers.

Answering children's questions presents excellent worship opportunities. Religious educators continue to emphasize that a child may learn more theology from the ages of two through six than he will ever learn again. That is, if parents attempt seriously to answer his questions: "What is the moon?" "If the sun is fire, why don't we burn up?" "What makes me sick?" "If grandmother went to be with God, why was she put in the ground?" "Where is God?" These are profound questions. The child literally drinks in the answers, catches attitudes, and develops convictions. Certainly intellectual comprehension is minimal, but this is not the important thing. The important thing is that the child is surrounded by an atmosphere of worship which makes the acceptance of these profound mysteries a natural thing.

3. The home as the center of worship should be bathed in a spirit of joy and happiness. A recent book which came to my desk contained a chapter, "A House Without a Home." The essence of the chapter was a large, beautiful house, set on the gentle slope of a hill. Everything about it was inviting. Yet unhappiness, sadness, and unloveliness was within. It was a house, but it was not a home.

In similar manner, little children may be given wrong ideas about God and even turned away from him if the religion (worship) of the home is that of sternness, repression, blind obedience, and fear. But a spirit of joy, happiness, and reverence for all things can capture the open innocence, freshness, and vitality of children and turn them Godward. It must be stressed that a happy, joyous religion helps children form positive attitudes.

4. The primary way in which the home may become a center of worship is through the living example of parents. Parents teach primarily through living—not through telling. Worship is caught through relationships. A child must witness the love of God in his parents. When he becomes confident that his parents' love is turned toward him, he grows into the confidence that God's love is the same. However, if the parents are undependable, unreliable, and unloving, then the child cannot develop an assurance that God and the universe are dependable.

What can a child think and feel toward a parent who lies in bed while the child is sent to Sunday School? Depth psychologists would point out that parents must practice in their own lives what they preach to their children, else the children may grow up with an unconscious hatred toward parents for not doing what they were forced to do. Parents who allow themselves to do things which they forbid the children to do, such as smoking, drinking, and dishonesty, are only laying the groundwork for such hatred.

It cannot be too strongly emphasized that the child develops his idea of God from the kind of nurture he receives as an infant. If he is going to develop a healthy love of God for himself, he must feel and witness the love of God in his parents or parent substitutes.

In summary, parents need to know that the child is not a miniature adult. Nor can he be prepared for adulthood by subjecting him to adult experiences. His background of experience (or lack of it), level of comprehension, interests, and needs are all different from those of an adult. It is only as the child lives fully and satisfyingly on the child level that he may be expected to grow into a fulfilled adulthood. Thus children who develop a sure and natural faith in God enjoy an advantage that lasts throughout their lifetime.

9

The Child and the Church

G. R. Beasley-Murray

The policy adopted by a church towards its members' children, and the place accorded to children generally in its ordered life, are determined by the view that is taken of the basic relationship which a child has to the church.

In many areas Christian people have but a vague notion as to what that relationship is. Where that is the case, it will be found that children are dealt with in a most haphazard manner; no one knows why they are doing what they are doing, nor are answers readily forthcoming when questions are asked. By contrast some groups have very clear ideas as to the relation of the child to the church, and in such cases their practice is equally clearly defined.

The Eastern Orthodox churches, for example, act with logical consistency on the basis of their view of baptism. Taking seriously the New Testament principle that baptism is to Christ and the church, they baptize infants and admit them at once to become full members of the church, entitled to participate freely in the privileges of Christian worship. The typical Orthodox service includes the communion service; little children therefore are permitted to attend the whole service of worship.

When the congregation moves forward to receive the bread and wine from the officiating priest, the little children are brought in their parents' arms to receive the elements. Once it is accepted that infant baptism is right this is a perfectly logical procedure, and it is difficult

127

to understand why other churches which practice infant baptism hesitate to follow the example of the Orthodox in this matter.

At the other end of the scale there are Baptists who virtually deny that children have any real place in the church at all. If they ever think to repudiate the term "adult" baptism as distinct from "believer's" baptism, they act as though adult baptism were the norm of Baptist life.

A well-known British Baptist minister in the first quarter of this century, P. T. Thomson by name, was struck by the prevalence of this attitude in Britain. He drew attention to a statement of a distinguished Baptist man of letters, Augustine Birrell, who wrote in his introduction to Boswell's *Life of Samuel Johnson,* "Children are all very well, but it is men and women who bear the burden of life and the heat of the day, and it is for them that literature was intended." Thomson suggested that if in that sentence "the church" were substituted for "literature," you have an apt expression of a characteristic attitude towards children in many Baptist churches: children are "all very well," but it was for men and women that the church was founded!

And the result of this view? P. T. Thomson expressed it as follows: "Children are never seen at what are known as church meetings; they are never present at the Communion Table; rarely in churches of the Baptist faith and order are they admitted to baptism; and, what is most significant of all, in many worship gatherings of the church, on occasion, it is difficult to discover the one or two exotic little mortals who seem to have found their way by accident into the enclosure reserved for middle age and beyond."

If that sounds strange to Baptist ears in the U.S.A., it is nevertheless all too often true of Baptist churches in Europe today. British Baptists would never consider permitting children to participate in the communion service, and they would be surprised to hear it suggested that children should ever be permitted to attend the monthly church business meetings. It is thereby assumed that Christ's church is a church of adults, and that children at best can only be prepared to join it after they have reached (or passed beyond) adolescence. The effect that this has on the life of the churches can easily be imagined—at least in Britain.

In contrast to this attitude, a famous theologian of the early centuries, Gregory Nazianzus, considered that children should be baptized and join the church at the age of three, for at that time some comprehension of the rite could be assumed. This was an interesting advance on the common custom of his day of applying baptism to infants a few days old, and Baptists have sometimes drawn attention to Gregory's views. It is even more interesting that there are Baptists today who are moving towards Gregory's position, in that they administer baptism to children of five and even four years of age (there were 1,146 such cases reported in Southern Baptist churches in 1966).

I learned recently of an application for *transfer* of membership from one Baptist church to another of a child four years of age. Startling as that sounds, the action is in strict accord with principle, where that principle is accepted; namely that baptism should be administered as soon as belief can be affirmed, irrespective of whether the person concerned be infant or aged. If this procedure were to be adopted among Baptists generally, it would have far-reaching effects on Baptist life, to say nothing of the relations of Baptists to other churches.

I am under the impression that on the whole Baptists are uncertain as to the relation of children to the church that is conformable to the Scriptures. They are uneasy about viewing the church as exclusively the church of adults, and they are equally uneasy at the idea of children being incorporated into full membership of the church when they are barely out of infancy (in Europe Baptists are astonished at the thought).

While our people naturally encourage their children to come to church, they are more used to thinking in terms of their children's relation to the Sunday School than to their relation to the church itself. I am fairly sure that it would not occur to most of them to think of their children as standing in any different relation to the church than anyone else's children do. Perhaps it is fair to say that Baptists are more concerned to affirm God's pity on the children of the heathen than they are to define his relation to their own children —they do not wish to give countenance to the idea that God penalizes children on account of their parentage.

Now while there laudable motives at work here, we must take care that we do not permit ourselves to substitute sentiment for straight thinking. For example, we need to face the unpleasant fact that almost all of the millions of children in China today are growing up without knowledge of God, of Christ, of the Bible, and of the church.

With few exceptions, they will shortly form the spearhead of a nation of pagans. They are in a very different position from the children of Christian families in North America who are growing up under the care of the church, learning of the love and power of God in Christ, and who will (we trust) shortly become the spearhead of the witnessing church.

To maintain that there is no difference between the children of the followers of Mao Tse-tung in Peking and the children of the followers of Jesus in Philadelphia in their respective relations to the church would be foolish. (Lest there be misunderstanding, let it be said that the comparison equally holds good between the children of the followers of Jesus in Peking and the children of mammon worshipers in Philadelphia!) Most of us believe that there is a difference between the church and the "world" (in the sense of John 15:18-19), but we strangely hesitate to recognize the effect of this difference on the children of believers and the children of people of the "world." The apostle Paul appeared to view this difference as axiomatic, and he referred to it as a self-evident point of reference from which one could advance to less certain matters.

I refer to the statement in 1 Corinthians that "the unbelieving husband is consecrated through his wife, and the unbelieving wife is consecrated through her husband. Otherwise, your children would be unclean, but as it is they are holy" (7:14, RSV). This saying had more or less fallen out of the Baptist Bible, but of late we have had to try to come to terms with it through the use made of it by proponents of infant baptism, and we find it difficult.

When Paul enunciated this statement, he had a different interest in view from ours. He wished to encourage a man or woman, converted to Christ since marriage but whose partner did not share the faith, to continue in the existing marriage relation. The Christian, he said, should not contemplate separation if the other partner was willing to remain, for the power of the Christian's sanctification is greater than that of the non-Christian's lack of holiness. This is demonstrated by a prior fact, which the apostle presumes all will acknowledge: if the case were so that the unbelieving partner defiled the Christian, then the defilement would extend to the children, but, as everybody knows, the contrary is true—*your children are holy!* This last clause is not deduced from the argument, rather it is a given datum from which a deduction is made concerning the non-Christian parent. The holiness of children belonging to Christian parents is axiomatic—even when only one parent is Christian.

Understandably a great deal of ink has been expended in endeavors to explain (or explain away) Paul's language, and I do not wish to use up more than is necessary here. Suffice it to say that Paul is drawing on terminology that is used in the Old Testament to describe Israel's relation to God and to other peoples. Israel has been taken from the world of nations to be "a kingdom of priests, and an holy nation" (Ex. 19:5-6). Israel, thus, is viewed as "holy," that is, belonging to God, just as the Temple in Jerusalem was "holy"; by contrast the rest of the world is "common," like the rest of the houses in Jerusalem. In terms of the ceremonial law, this may be expressed by saying that Israel is "clean," over against a world that is "unclean."

In Paul's day, when converts from paganism to Judaism were becoming increasingly frequent, the rabbis made a special point of impressing this distinction on their converts. They even drew a line between the children of a convert born before the convert's entry into Judaism and those born afterwards. The former were said to be not born "in holiness," and so were unclean, since they were born in heathenism; the latter were viewed as born "in holiness," and so were clean, because they were born Jews.

The analogy with Paul's language is evident: the church is heir to the promises of God and may rightly be described as the Israel of God (Gal. 6:16), the true people of God; therefore to be in it is to be in the sphere of holiness over against the unclean world. The family of a Christian man or woman is "clean" through the relation of the believing parent to Christ and the church, and this sanctification is said even to embrace the non-Christian partner.

Paul's argument goes far beyond anything any rabbi was prepared to acknowledge. For the rabbis would have said that, on the contrary, the uncleanness of the pagan partner would defile the convert, and so they did not allow a married person to enter Judaism as a convert without the partner. Paul denies this traditional position, for he works on the basis that a part sanctifies the whole (cf. Rom. 11:16, where he teaches that the godly remnant in the nation Israel preserves the true nature of Israel and gives hope that the whole nation will be converted at the last). Paul gives the encouraging thought that it might even be possible that the power of Christian holiness should at length break down the non-Christian's resistance to the gospel and lead him or her to Christ. (Cf. 1 Cor. 7:16, NEB, which reads, "Think of it: as a wife you may be your husband's salvation; as a husband you may be your wife's salvation.")

Now it is to be admitted that this is a way of thinking to which we are not accustomed, and it is unusual for Paul also to employ these categories drawn from the ancient Levitical laws. For this reason we must distinguish between his use of terms like "consecrate" and "holiness" in 1 Corinthians 7:14, RSV, from the meaning he gives them when they relate to the transforming experience of redemption in Christ and the Holy Spirit.

Nevertheless by use of ancient terminology of the ceremonial law Paul has found a method of expressing the way in which a Christian's family is important to God. He indicates that *the relation of such a family to God and the church marks it off from the godless world.* Contrary to our tendency to draw black and white distinctions between those in the church and those out of it, Paul suggests that it is possible to come within the sphere of the church's blessing without actually being a confessed member. And of course this applies, above all, to the children of believers.

The importance of this will be immediately apparent, but it is not only Baptists who have been slow to recognize it. Having in view the Baptist reluctance to admit infants and very young children into church membership, D. M. Baillie, in *The Theology of the Sacraments,* asked whether the children of Christians are to be regarded as having a place in the church or whether they are to be viewed as outsiders. Are they children of God or children of wrath, Christian children or little pagans? To these rather shocking questions he believed the answer was plain: It is God's will that our children should experience his grace as children, and that they should be seen as part of the church, the entrance to which is through baptism.

These words of Baillie's have been frequently quoted as though they dealt a devastating blow to Baptist beliefs, but the issue is not so simple. Baptists also believe that God wills that children should grow up from their earliest days in the knowledge of his love, and that they should experience the gracious influences of the church's fellowship. But the oppositions posed by Baillie between insiders and outsiders, children of God and children of wrath, little Christians and little pagans, could not apply to Paul's view of the relation to the church of the families of believers. Nor indeed could Baillie's suggestion that children of Christian parents come into their position of "holiness" through being baptized as infants. For the blessing of the Christian's sanctification in 1 Corinthians 7:14 extends to the non-Christian partner as well as to the children, and manifestly he or she has not been baptized!

It would seem that the apostolic church viewed the children of Christian parents as standing in a unique relation to the church. They were not regarded as born-again children of God for such an experience must await the opening of the life to Christ in faith. But neither were these children regarded as part of the world that lies in the power of the evil one (1 John 5:19). They were seen rather as lying under the care of God, in the bosom of the church, committed by the Lord to its tender care and nurture, in hope of their ultimate entry into the life of faith in Christ.

It will be noted that our discussion has assumed a peculiarly close relation between the Christian family and the church. The child of Christian parents is related to the church through the parents who are members of it. Yet the "sanctity" or holiness of the household is due to the family's connection with the church (ultimately, of course, to Christ in the church). The responsibility for the unfolding of the spiritual potential of the children therefore rests alike on the parents and the church, just as the gracious influences of the Holy Spirit are felt in the Christian home and in the church. This duality of responsibility and opportunity of home and church to be instruments of the grace of God in the life of the child should be impressed on both parents and local church.

The desire to achieve this latter end has given rise to the custom of the so-called "dedication service" among some groups of Baptists, especially in England. Perhaps a word of explanation may be profitable at this point, in view of the misunderstandings to which the custom has given rise.

That Christian parents should bring their newborn children to church to give thanks to God for them and to seek the blessing of God on them seems natural enough. Similarly most people feel it right to seek God's blessing on a marriage among the fellowship of his people, and to seek his blessing when they walk in the valley of the shadow of death.

The term "dedication service," however, is questionable, and many prefer to speak of a "service for the presentation and blessing of infants." On such an occasion it is desired to give thanks to the Creator for the gift of life and for the provision of a redemption that has included in its sweep this little child. Prayer is offered for the blessing of God on the child and that through the efforts of parents and church the child may learn of Christ and respond to his grace in the fellowship of the church.

To bring home this responsibility, questions are addressed first to the parents and then to the church. The parents are asked whether they pledge themselves to bring up their child in the ways of God, to encourage him to read the Scriptures and to pray, and so at length to help him make his own confession of faith in Christ. The church is asked whether it accepts its responsibility to train the child in the knowledge of God, encourage him in worship, show him Christ's love, and help him to confess Christ as Lord. On suitable responses being given to these questions, a declaration like the following is made: "In gratitude to God and in dependence on him, we solemnly commit you to the nurture and admonition of the Lord, praying that as he has graciously given you life in this world he may early give you the life of his eternal kingdom."

There is admittedly little scriptural authority for an action of this kind (the presentation of Jesus in the Temple, Luke 2:22, was for a different purpose), but it does bring home in a touching manner the responsibility of parents and church for their little ones, and their dependence on the Lord for carrying out this aspect of his commission to them.

Experience proves that we constantly need reminding of this responsibility, for if we fail in our families we fail at the nearest and most crucial point of our mission. Where a custom of this kind does not exist it is eminently desirable that parents and congregation should be reminded from time to time of the crucial importance of this element of their commission from the Lord. No one has given more striking example of this concern than did Jesus himself: "Let the children come to me . . . for to such belongs the kingdom of God" (Mark 10:14, RSV), or the terrible warning, "Whoever causes one of these little ones who believe in me to sin, it would be better for him if a great millstone were hung round his neck and he were thrown into the sea" (Mark 9:42, RSV). The church that claims to continue the work of the Saviour in the world must not fail to perpet-uate it among its own children.

So far we have thought mainly of the relation of the very young child to the church; how are we to conceive of the relation of the growing child to the church? I think we have a clue in Paul's refer-ence to the duty of fathers to bring up their children in the "nurture and admonition of the Lord," as the King James Version puts it (Eph. 6:4). The Revised Standard Version renders that phrase "the discipline and instruction of the Lord," *The New English Bible,* "the instruction, and the correction, which belong to a Christian upbring-ing."

Now there was in the ancient church an institution for carrying out that function, and it came to be known as the catechumenate. The word was derived from a Greek verb meaning to instruct, and it sim-ply denoted the position of those who were under instruction in the Christian faith. From its earliest days the church instructed the new converts, and like Israel, from which it sprang, it extended this instruction to the children of its members. A comparison of the teaching of the New Testament Epistles with the traditional instruc-tion which Jews gave to converts from heathenism shows that the early church copied much of the Jewish teaching.

In the earliest years, instruction was given to converts after their baptism and entry into the church (all the baptisms recorded in Acts took place immediately after the converts professed faith in Christ, as on the day of Pentecost, the conversion of the centurion, Cornelius, and his friends, and the Philippian jailer). It is probable that later the instruction was set partly *before* baptism and partly *after* admission to church membership. We know that in due course it came to be placed almost entirely *before* baptism, and that it usually continued for a period of three years. When people talk about the catechumen-ate, they usually have in mind the developed form that it came to take, and they specifically have in view the period between an inquir-er's acceptance for Christian instruction and his baptism.

A candidate for the catechumenate was questioned as to his motives for wishing to be enrolled. He would then be given some ele-mentary teaching and asked if he really believed it. If it appeared that he was fit to proceed further, he was formally initiated as a "catechu-men." People who were so initiated formed a recognized group within the church; they were allowed to attend the services of worship, but they were not permitted to remain for the Lord's Supper. Their position therefore was an ambiguous one. They had stepped out of the godless world, but they were not yet numbered with the saints; they were on the way to inclusion in the church, somewhat like Israel after leaving Egypt, traveling through the desert to the Promised Land.

It will be appreciated that the position of the young child who is being "disciplined" unto Christ is different from that of the adult inquirer who asks to be prepared for baptism and church membership. But the analogy is also clear: the child in the care of the church and learning Christ's way is not in the "world," nor is he strictly "in" the church, in the sense of being incorporated into the body of Christ. He is on the way, like his older brother who seeks to know Christ and be numbered with the elect—on the way to confession of Christ in baptism, on the way to becoming one of Christ's representatives in the world. Here is the most important point: the child of the church is being cared for and instructed in the faith. In time the life that is nurtured issues in new birth, and being so regenerated it begins to assume a mode of life that befits a responsible member of the people of God.

The process and the goal are alike important. We must be clear that the process is more than the impartation of religious knowledge, and the goal is more than the production of a good character. The process is the patient exposition of "the whole counsel of God" in the Scriptures, the goal is the child's acceptance and its translation into life through the confession of Christ in his church and following in his steps in the world.

This process and goal are well defined by J. D. Smart in *The Teaching Ministry of the Church*: "Our goal must be no lesser goal than that which Jesus and the apostles had before them. We teach so that through our teaching God may work in the hearts of those whom we teach to make of them disciples wholly committed to his gospel, with an understanding of it, and with a personal faith that will enable them to bear convincing witness to it in word and action in the midst of an unbelieving world. We teach so that through our teaching God may bring into being a Church whose glory will be the fullness with which God indwells it in his love and truth and power, and whose all-engrossing aim will be to serve Jesus Christ as an earthly body through which he may continue his redemption of the world."

This is a valuable statement from Smart, since it conjoins teaching the gospel with discipleship, church, and mission. It provides a welcome correction of a strangely fashionable tendency among some theologians today to belittle the church of Christ—as though God can be served better out of the church than in it, and better without the church than with it!

We do well to remember, however, that there can be no gospel for the world without the body of Christ to proclaim it. The Gospel must bring people into the body of Christ if the gospel is to produce its God-intended result. It was this that the missionary statesman Godfrey Phillips had in mind when he defined the church's task as "the transmission of Christian faith and life." He added in explanation: "Without divine activity no divine society, without the divine society no record, and no transmission. We hand on what we have received, not by dropping books out of the blue sky, but by transplanting the Church whose life, created by the acts of the God they relate, shows what they really mean."

If that holds good with regard to converts from without the church, it is equally true of children nurtured by the church. Our aim with respect to them is the encouragement of a ready response to the Word through a free and full commitment to Christ and his church.

What role does baptism play in this process and goal of instruction? In the scheme of the ancient catechumenate, baptism so completely formed the goal of the process that instruction largely ceased when the goal was reached. The catechumenate gave place to membership in the church. This pattern has been commonly followed in modern foreign missions of all denominations, and fundamentally the same applies to most Baptist groups in Europe, whether the period of instruction extends to three weeks, three months, or three years. Unfortunately there are Baptist groups wherein it is not thought needful to provide the young in faith with *any* instruction at the time of baptism. I am convinced, on the contrary, that such instruction is necessary for the sake of the church's health and that of its individual members. So instruction concerns not simply baptism as a rite, but Christian doctrine and Christian life.

I am constrained to ask why it should be thought appropriate that this instruction should only precede baptism and cease at that point. Surely there is a need for the young to be both prepared for baptism —in spiritual fitness and in its significance for life and faith, and for them to be rooted and grounded afterwards in the faith, life, worship, and service of the church. Baptism should not be regarded as the conclusion of Christian instruction, but rather as the pivotal point, the critical event which gives meaning to it all. It is the point to which the prior training and instruction move and for which they exist. It is the occasion from which they move forward, as the believer who has entered on to his birthright in Christ seeks to grow in grace, in knowledge, in responsible living, and in the service of Christ in the church and the world.

The fitting age at which this event should take place has been discussed elsewhere in this book, but it is hardly possible to be silent on the issue in the context of our discussion. Our concern in this article is with the *child* in the church, not with the wider subject of *man* in the church. We have seen that the child in the church is in a unique position. Doubtless it is the glory of the gospel that Christ can meet a man's need at any stage of his life, even when he has sunk to the deepest pit of hell on earth, and the church is sent by its Lord to seek the lost of every age in every place.

It is equally true, however, that the church should make every effort to prevent the children of its families from sinking into the sort of situation in which the Philippian jailer found himself—in middle life in an earthquake and about to commit suicide, before he had the opportunity to ask, "What must I do to be saved?" We have ground for hope that through the intercessions of family and church, and the children's participation in worship and instruction at home and in church, they may be spared the prodigal's bitter experience in the far country and respond in their early years to the love of God in Christ.

There are the best of reasons for refraining from subjecting little children to evangelistic pressures designed for awakening the consciences of hardened sinners. But we should also beware of underestimating the ability of a growing child to respond to the gospel and to grasp the essential significance for life.

In Britain the parting of the ways for a child's education has for years been the age of eleven, at which time serious application to classical and modern languages is widely begun and the process of learning is stepped up in all fields. In face of this, it is strange how commonly churches doubt a child's ability to think on the meaning of Christ for him, although he has to apply his mind to new realms of thought and experience every working day at school. Further, there is

The Child and the Church 139

a serious theological factor to be taken into account in the context of our discussion.

Warren Carr has rightly pointed out that the child of Christian parents, growing up under the ministry of the church, is in an analogous position to a child in ancient Israel. He is, in fact, in the tradition of the "New Israel." In itself this serves as a reminder that continued instruction in religious life and doctrine without the experience of grace tends to have a legalistic effect upon a person, even as it did in ancient Judaism.

In *Baptism: Conscience and Clue for the Church,* Carr writes: "Postponement of baptism, until adolescence or later maturity, for those who have been influenced by the dominant motif of Christian education is unwise. The individual under these conditions will probably be religiously structured so that he will be sinfully proud of his 'theological faith' and his 'legalistic goodness.' This structure can become so rigid as to desensitize him to a gospel of grace."

Carr considers therefore that a child nurtured in the church should receive baptism at such time as his response to the gospel is clear. Relating this to the "catechumenate" he writes: "A child's baptism ought not mark the final event in his Christian education. Instead, it should be an interruption of the Christian education so that the child may respond, personally and accountably, to God's grace which has been presupposed throughout the process. This interruption has to be consciously perceived. Grace, already given in the death, burial, and resurrection of Christ, needs to be symbolized in an event that may be continuously remembered by the child. Baptism is the event and Christian education provides the memory and recall that is necessary.

I am increasingly of the opinion that we should do all that is legitimate and right to mark the importance of confession of faith and baptism for the life of the young believer. Since the New Testament teaches that baptism is for Christ and the church, we should make that explicit by welcoming the baptized into the membership of the church at his baptism.

There are indications in the New Testament that the custom of laying on hands at baptism was frequent, perhaps universal (see Acts 19:6 and Heb. 6:2). Some early Baptists attached great importance to this, and I think with justice, though I would not wish to make an undue issue of it. For laying on of hands is a time-honored symbol from earliest biblical times of prayer for the blessing of God. In the

New Testament times, it was used symbolically for commissioning Christian workers (Acts 13:2-3). To make baptism the consecration of the baptized to the service of Christ in the church and in the world would be entirely in accord with the meaning of the Christian life, and it would aid in putting it into effect.

Lastly, the ancient church used to conclude every baptismal service with a communion service—the first one in which the newly baptized participated. This, too, had the effect of marking the importance of the entrance of the convert into the membership of the church and its privileges, and I see no reason why this should not be revived among us. (I forbear to launch on reasons why we *ought* to revive it!)

In view of the importance of the baptismal event to the life of a child reared in the church, I would conclude by raising the issue as to who should participate in the instruction of the child. Manifestly we ought to be able to take it for granted that Christian parents in their home will encourage their child in the Christian life. Ideally they will help to establish him or her in devotional habits (the reading of the Bible and prayer) and in some reading concerning our faith and the exploits of those whose lives have been inspired by it. The Sunday School provides a continuous and systematic medium of instruction in the Christian faith, especially the Bible, and on the Sunday School a great burden of responsibility rests.

If we are candid, however, I think we have to recognize that in practice both parents and Sunday School teachers frequently fall short of the requirements of really adequate instruction, above all in connection with the crisis time of baptism. I would earnestly suggest therefore that the pastor or someone trained specifically should assume responsibility for a continuing orientation class for inquirers and young Christians. There are two advantages in this.

First, those who have become aware of the wonder of Christ's redemption and turn to the Lord for his salvation naturally want to know more about its meaning and its significance for their lives. They are therefore ready to give more earnest consideration to Christian doctrine and the Christian view of life than they are at ordinary times. If, in fact, their enthusiasm in this regard is not conspicuous, it ought not to be difficult to rouse their consciences as to the necessity for special instruction at the time of baptism. This would do much to establish young believers in their newly embraced faith and would help them to see its implications for life.

Second, every pastor knows how difficult it is at times to be confident that a young person asking for baptism is in earnest about responding to the grace of God in Christ and making a true commitment of life. (The difficulty, in fact, is not confined to the young; there are all sorts of secondary reasons that can operate in an older person's mind in requesting baptism, and he is more skilled at covering them up than the child!) If there is a continuing instruction class, such difficulties may be discovered and relieved. The individual can be baptized at such time as it seems evident that his profession of faith is real—and they will continue in the instruction till they have concluded the course.

Admittedly it places a burden on the minister to arrange such a class. However, the issue is so important, and the significance it could have for the health of the church, it would be worth the minister's setting aside some of his less important tasks to see that this one is done properly. It is good when a minister can echo the words of Paul to the members of a church he had founded: "The lessons I taught you, the tradition I have passed on, all that you heard me say or saw me do, put into practice; and the God of peace will be with you" (Phil. 4:9, NEB).

10

Moving in the Right Direction
Clifford Ingle

Where are we going? Perhaps a review of the material presented thus far will be helpful to our efforts to suggest some possible solutions.

Chapter 1 is an attempt to set out the confusion and the concern of both individuals and denominations over the religious status of the child and his relationship to the church. One Southern Baptist theologian said that in his opinion this subject is the crossroads, not only of theology and psychology, but also of our understanding of sin and salvation. The vital nature of this subject is shown by his prediction that the religious status of the child will be the major topic of discussion among Christian theologians during the next several years.

Writers of Sunday School materials are already facing this issue and making serious reappraisals of the content, format, and grading of the materials. Church members are pleading earnestly that we tell them whether or not what they and the churches believe and are doing is wrong; and if it is, they want someone to tell them what is right. This book is a serious attempt to begin the search for answers to these questions.

The teachings and implications of the Old Testament would suggest the following truths concerning any attempted formulation of a theology of children and the church: (1) children entered into and were members of the covenant community through corporate identity with their father; (2) religious instruction and worship were carried on in the home with the father as the teacher; (3) from birth the

142

child was a member of the covenant community and only a personal repudiation of the covenant could break his membership, which act was considered to be one of illegitimacy and dishonor. Only those outside the covenant community faced the question of whether or not to accept the God of Israel. These were referred to as proselytes. Thus the only option for a native Israelite was not the acceptance of his faith, but its rejection. There was no "once-for-all" decision to be made or a time when he assumed covenant obligations.

The New Testament is marked by a sparsity of teachings on the subject of children as participants of the Christian faith. In the Gospels, Jesus' references to children served primarily as object lessons designed to illustrate the meaning of his good news for adults. Therefore, the Gospels tell us nothing of significance about how to evangelize children or how to educate them within the framework of the Christian faith.

The only passage in the book of Acts which refers directly to children (21:5) draws a clear distinction between believers and their children. The implication is that the believers did not think of their own children as participants in the Christian fellowship.

In the Epistles, all references to children deal in some way with the life of the family, not with the relation of children to the church. Yet in Ephesians and Colossians Paul indicated that the children of Christian homes must recognize that the pattern of their own life is an essential aspect of the Christian life of the home. This, however, still leaves us with no discernible directions on how children are to be incorporated into the life of the church.

These truths remind us that if we are to find adequate directions for the solution of the problems which we face in trying to relate our children to Christ and to the church, we must be dependent upon the Holy Spirit's leadership, which Jesus promised to his disciples. The great question for us, then, is whether or not we are willing to enter into a dynamic venture of the Spirit in order to walk the road which God would have us follow. After all, Jesus' promise of continuous presence with his people was contingent upon their walking with him over unfamiliar paths.

Chapter 4 points out two areas of special problems for Baptists in our work of child evangelism. Much unbiblical thinking in these two areas must be altered if our work with children is to be done in a way which is in keeping with the New Testament. First, we must remember that the Bible, particularly Romans 5:12-21 does *not* teach that babies are born sinners. Paul's doctrine of sin is found in Romans 1:18-3:26, in which he shows sin to be the problem of man acting in enlightened freedom. He knows that there are things which he should not do, but he chooses to do them anyway. *All* are sinners, not because of guilt inherited from Adam, but because all choose to rebel against God as they know him.

Second, we must remember that salvation is much more than going to heaven, rather than to hell, after the death of the body. Eternal life is, first, a life of conscious fellowship with God in Jesus Christ (John 16:3). He who has this life gives his purposed and conscious obedience to Christ as his Lord. This freely-followed pattern of life is available only to the person who has come to an awareness of self and of the meaning of selfhood. Such awareness comes to people at differing ages in life, but very few experience that insight before adolescence.

In chapter 5 we saw that Baptist thought did not begin in a vacuum. Many prior theological currents have helped to shape their teachings. Whatever position one may hold with regard to salvation and to the relation of children to the church, he must examine his reasons for that position in the light of church history. Such history represents the attempts of the people of God to interpret and understand the will of God in their time.

Christian literature of the first two centuries reveals that while the early followers of Christ took their children to their meetings, neither infants nor young children were baptized. Infant baptism, confirmation, and the catechumenate arose during the third century. Infant baptism was based upon the presupposition that it washed away original sin inherited from Adam. Such baptism admitted the infant into the household of faith. Confirmation, which involved anointing with oil and laying on of hands, seemingly signified the priesthood of the individual. The catechumenate arose as a result of the spread of Christianity into non-Jewish lands where the people had no Old Testament or Judaistic background. It was a period of probation lasting up to three years in which the catechumen (person requesting baptism) was instructed in the faith.

During the Middle Ages infant baptism and confirmation became accepted practices in Catholic, Lutheran, and Reformed churches, with each group offering varying explanations as to their meaning and purpose. Due to the influence of those who favored the "gathered church," which should be composed of baptized believers only, there arose various splinter groups, such as Anabaptists, Mennonites, Congregationalists, General and Particular Baptists, and others. As these widely scattered individuals and groups developed into churches and denominations, two principles seem to stand out: First, baptism of believers only. Infant baptism was rejected although most groups retained sprinkling and pouring, along with immersion, as valid modes of baptism. Second, the form of church government was congregational or democratic.

Chapter 6 took up the difficult problem of accountability which refers to that period in life when one is sufficiently aware of God through grace to decide for or against Christ. This is based upon the demands of biblical faith which is the same for all persons. That is, there is no such thing as a gospel for children and one for adults. Thus accountability must be related to one's ability to grasp and accept the basic truths of the gospel.

What are these truths? The first is a recognition of sin as separation from God. One cannot be saved until he is aware he is lost. Second, there must be a knowledge of who Jesus is and what he has done on our behalf, that his death for all men is followed by his resurrection, and that God's Spirit draws men to God. Third, in addition to hearing and believing these facts, each individual must have a faith in Jesus Christ which is accompanied by repentance from a former way of life.

Can a child understand, believe, and accept these things? This depends on the child, his ability, his age, maturation, and capacity to grasp thoughts and make decisions. It depends upon his family, his church, and the language used to express these ideas. If we mean, can a child of nine or ten understand and express the basic truths necessary for conversion in adult terms the answer is no. An important biblical truth is that God speaks to each individual at his own level.

However, this does not mean that all one needs to do to become a Christian is to say, "I love Jesus." There is a core of understanding which is essential to salvation for any age because that core is the basis or center of a new life. Little children may be led to express commitments to God beyond their capacity to understand or to decide—and do this in adult language. The covenant of grace between God and man gives us every reason to believe that children are kept by God until they can make meaningful and understandable decisions for themselves.

Strange as it may seem, it is only within recent years that Baptist religious educators have given serious recognition to the moral and religious growth and understanding of children as a theological concern. Too long the emphasis has been upon "saving the soul" without proper regard for the God-given and God-directed processes of intellect, emotion, and behavior. Yet these are vital elements in the wholeness or unity of each person.

In chapter 7 the author emphasizes that any theology of children must include a recognition and understanding of these developmental processes. Otherwise a child may be pushed into making religious decisions which he does not understand and which in later years he may reject. Or he may possess a hazy notion of Christianity that is little more than superstition.

Some specific ideas which must play a role in understanding and developing a theology of children are: (1) A child must experience (feel) before he can understand; so teaching is more through example, attitude, and activity than through factual knowledge. (2) Individual differences must be recognized. No one should expect all children to develop morally, socially, religiously, intellectually, and emotionally at the same rate or according to a set pattern.

(3) Recent studies of intellectual abilities have proved that many widely accepted concepts are false, particularly the idea of measurement by the intelligence quotient and the assumption that intellectual capacity and ability are fixed. Researchers are now saying it is possible to vary the IQ as much as thirty points; so intelligence is to be viewed as flexible and dynamic. (4) Moral and religious growth and understanding should be recognized as a part of normal development in all of its aspects. Religious thinking is not some special or separate mode of thought, but is a process of thinking identical with that which is exercised in other fields. This is in accord with God's total creative work.

The one basic theological fact concerning the child and the home set in chapter 8 is that parents or parent substitutes are the first and most important teachers of religion. This is true regardless of the religious status of the parents or parent substitutes. They may be good or bad, believers or unbelievers, faithful or unfaithful Christians and church members; yet they are the first humans known to the child. They teach what they are! Such teaching is accomplished more by attitude, action, and example than by factual information. It is conveyed primarily through living—not through telling.

Thus the child develops his idea of God from the kind of nurture he receives. If he is going to experience his own healthy love of God, he must feel and witness the love of God in his parents or parent substitutes. Churches and denominational agencies should prepare the materials necessary to insure a total home ministry. This includes premarital as well as postmarital training.

In chapter 9 the author states that the place accorded to children in the life of the church is determined by the views taken by the members concerning the relationship which the church has with the child. Most Baptists do not know what that relationship should be and as a result are probably more inconsistent in dealing with children than is any other major denomination. However the author quickly points out that having clear ideas and practices concerning the relation of the child to the church does not mean that such ideals and practices are scriptural. The author interprets Paul (1 Cor. 7:14) and the apostolic churches as seeing the children of Christian parents as having a unique relationship to the church. That is, they were committed by Christ to the care and nurture of the church in hope of their ultimate entry into the church through personal faith in Christ. This means that both home and church as instruments of God's grace are directly responsible for the spiritual life of the child.

Two specific suggestions are offered concerning this accomplishment: (1) A service of blessing or dedication of new life in which the parents present the infant before the church to bless God for the new life and to hear a charge to both parents and church. Both pledge themselves to bring up the child in the ways of God, so that in due time he will make his own confession of faith and continue to grow in Christian maturity. (Some Baptist pastors conduct such a service in the home or at the hospital.)

(2) The church should recognize each child as a catechumen—one who is being instructed. In reality this instruction is to begin in the home and the Preschool Dept., and is to continue into adulthood. The goal of such instruction is to nurture the child in the ways of God, leading him to respond personally and accountably to God's grace in

salvation. However, the new birth, baptism, and church membership should not be regarded as final events, but as necessary milestones in the process of becoming into the "fulness" of Christ.

What About Infant Baptism?

Today as a spirit of renewal, goodwill, and ecumenicity is being encouraged among Christian bodies, serious attention is being given to those doctrines and practices which separate us. Interestingly enough, one of the major differences is infant baptism. It may come as a surprise to most Baptists to learn that infant baptism is practiced by the majority of Christian bodies. The assumption among those who practice it is that those who do not, including Baptists, are wrong. Specifically, this suggests that a major difference among Christian groups would be settled if Baptists and others who limit baptism to believers only would change their position on this matter.

While Baptists would admit to confusion concerning the relation of children to God and the church, it does not follow that those who practice infant baptism are right or that they are not confused.

Historically, the practice of infant baptism arose as a serious attempt to solve the problem of the status of the newborn child. Since the time of Augustine (A.D. 354-430) the great majority of Christendom has met this problem by assuming that the child inherited the sin of Adam's transgression (Adamic sin, guilt). The child was thereby damned (lost), and it was through baptism (usually sprinkling) that they were cleansed of inherited guilt and were delivered into the kingdom of God. An example of this teaching clearly set forth by the Roman Catholic Church is that because of inherited or original sin children are lost, and if they die before baptism they will be forever shut out of the bliss of heaven.

Today this doctrine has been modified in varying degrees by those who believe a form of it. Yet the belief in the need of the infant to be cleansed from inherited sin and/or guilt and that baptism is God's means of accomplishing this cleansing are still maintained. For example, the Church of England views confirmation as the completion of the meaning of baptism, teaching that a child is regenerated at baptism by the act of God. However, the child needs to be converted by surrendering his will to God. Thus the Church of England sees in confirmation what Baptists see in conversion.

During the Reformation some of the church leaders rejected the doctrine upon which infant baptism was founded but retained infant baptism by substituting the idea that such baptism was analogous to circumcision. That is, just as circumcision is a sign forever (Gen. 17:9-14) that Israel is God's chosen people, so infants of Christian parents have been born directly into the inheritance of the covenant and are to be received through the seal of baptism into the kingdom of God and unto future repentance and faith.

To Baptists the practice of infant baptism for any reason is a serious error based upon assumptions which are unwarranted. The writer remembers most vividly an experience which he had while serving as a chaplain during World War II. He was asked to go to the hospital to baptize an infant whose life was in doubt. Upon securing a chaplain of the same faith as the parents of the child, the writer asked for the privilege of witnessing the baptism. He listened as the liturgy for the baptism of infants was read and he observed as the chaplain dipped one finger in water and touched it to the baby's forehead. It was then that the writer determined to begin a serious study of infant baptism, which study has continued to the present time.

Ultimately, the reasons given for such practice can be summarized under the idea found in the New Testament of household baptism (see the excellent discussion of this in chapter 4) and that nowhere in the Scriptures is infant baptism denied. To reason that the Bible teaches infant baptism because it does not deny it is a speculation from silence that can be neither proved nor disproved. Such an approach is as false as that followed by some European theologians who assume the Bible is false until proved true; and since you cannot prove it true, then it is false.

Today, serious questions as to the validity of infant baptism are being raised by some theologians or religious bodies practicing it. For example, a Methodist bishop in speaking to the faculty and student body of Midwestern Baptist Theological Seminary stated that infant baptism had no scriptural basis and should be abandoned, and that the ministers of his bishopric and fellow bishops had been told by him of his position on the subject.

Our argument with those who practice infant baptism is not that they seek to make a place for the child in the life of the church. We, too, seek to do that, and we, too, may be confused as to how this is done. Our argument is that they wrongly transfer to the beginning of life that which follows the new birth experience. Thus baptism is given a meaning, significance, and mode contrary to the teachings of the New Testament.

Suggested Approaches

Suggested approaches and practices among Baptists in dealing with children in relation to conversion and the church are many and varied. At one extreme are those who insist that conversion is a miracle of grace in the life of the individual, and a little child of five or six years of age may just as easily experience such a work of grace as an adult. Usually, the argument is that if the Holy Spirit has led the child to "come forward," what right have we to question such action?

Those who oppose such a position say it is contrary to the principles of normal growth and development of a child and also to the operation of the Holy Spirit. To attribute actions to the Holy Spirit which defy all principles of God's orderly activity in his created universe is to place upon God our own preconceived ideas as to his operation in the lives of people contrary to the best evidence from the Scriptures as well as human experience.

At the other extreme are those who insist that true discipleship is an adult experience. They feel it is impossible to have such an experience until one reaches the time of renouncing an "inherited faith," passed through a period of "doubt," and comes to that place of maturity where thoughts, decisions, and actions are his own. Such a time is usually not reached until later adolescence (16-19 years of age). Those who maintain such a position argue that it is only at such a time that one's thinking has matured sufficiently to permit the individual to be a responsible person in his own right. Such maturity and responsibility is necessary for church membership.

This argument is further strengthened according to its followers by pointing out that the greatest loss in our churches is the loss of teenagers. Also they point to such inconsistencies as children, ages six through 11, being received into "full" church membership and having the privilege of voting on all church matters—even such vital matters as calling a pastor, the church budget, and matters of discipline. Well does the writer remember a business meeting in which the church was voting on calling a pastor. Members of a large family who never attended midweek services had obviously been "canvassed" to be present and vote the "correct" way. Three of the children, all under twelve—yet members of the church, showed their ballots to their parents for a verification that they had voted properly.

Many who maintain this position insist that if a church does receive individuals at an earlier age, then baptism and church membership should be withheld until the proper time of "responsible maturity."

Those who disagree with this position believe that it places too much emphasis upon the intellectual grasping of abstract concepts which is but one part of the total self. They also point out that to wait until later adolescence is to go beyond the time when the child is naturally "bent" toward religion and open to God's leadership. It is also to deny the child the power of God at the most crucial time in his life.

An approach which is beginning to be studied and accepted in some churches is based upon the idea that children of Christian parents have a special relationship to God and the church and that the parents, the child, and the church should know this. Such a relationship should be emphasized within the life of the church.

Dr. William E. Hull introduces a plan based upon this idea in saying that the statements most children make when presenting themselves for church membership may be summarized as: (1) they love Jesus and desire to follow him; (2) they wish to belong to the church of their parents; (3) they want to be baptized because this is what they are supposed to do. While these statements may be important, they are not the essence of New Testament conversion. For example, how can a child on the basis of such a decision experience the meaning of lostness, Christ's death, and the putting off the old man with the lusts thereof, and "seek those things which are above"?

Dr. Hull believes that Baptists can have a positive and sound theology to which a child may respond. Such theology is based on the covenant idea of the Old Testament, which understood that the child was born into the community of the people of God, and the teachings of Paul, which affirmed that the children of a believing parent are "holy" in the solidarity of a Christian family (1 Cor. 7:14). He suggests three steps in such a process, steps in keeping with the best evidence of religious psychologists and biblical theology as to a child's search for a mature faith.

1. *A service of dedication or blessing.*—Such services are informal and usually conducted as a part of a worship service. The parents

with the infant present themselves before the church. During the brief ceremony the parents and church are called upon to recognize that life is the gift of God and that the little child is accepted by God as an individual in his own right. The parents and the church are asked to vow solemnly before God that this new life will be accepted as the responsibility of parents and church to be nurtured in the Lord until the time of responsible decision. Both parents and church may rest assured that the child is secure in the love of God until an understanding of estrangement (lostness) and need for salvation is felt and understood.

Whatever one's feeling may be concerning such a practice, one thing is sure: the Old Testament makes clear the importance of family faith, that is, being born into the chosen people of God. The apostle Paul emphasizes the great significance of acknowledging that a child has been born into a Christian home. Now it needs to be made clear that in no way can this be construed as a "new birth experience." This comes later—at the time of responsible decision.

2. *As the child grows, it is important for him to be reminded of his heritage and be given the opportunity to accept this heritage for himself.*—The implications and acceptance of this heritage could come during ages of six through eleven in some form of meaningful service. Let it be emphasized that this is not to be confused with the conversion experience. It is an accepted acknowledgment on the part of the growing child of his Christian heritage and his affirmation of his desire to love Jesus and continue in his ways.

It may be of interest at this point to see how one leader in the Roman Catholic Church approaches the matter of children and the church. Soon after becoming the bishop of Rochester, New York, Fulton J. Sheen announced that the age of confirmation in his diocese would be raised from the ages nine through eleven to that of normal high school graduation. The bishop explained his action by saying he was being asked to confirm tots as soldiers of Christ and to send them into the world before they were ready to be lay priests in the world (*Time,* February 24, 1967, p. 72).

However, Bishop Sheen saw that such a move could impoverish earlier childhood experiences; thus he suggested adding a new, unnamed ceremony for the young in the form of a renewal of the baptismal vows made on their behalf at infancy.

This example is given to show that regardless of the doctrinal differences between Roman Catholics and Baptists, Bishop Sheen was struggling with that which is also a Baptist problem, because at its depth it is a human problem.

3. *Conversion, baptism, and church membership.*—As the individual moves from childhood into youth, he moves from an inherited or borrowed faith into the struggle for a faith of his own. He moves from parental protection and acceptance of parental decisions to personal autonomy. He comes to see that his sins are not primarily against parents and friends but against God. In his outreach for adulthood, he experiences doubt, estrangement, and guilt, which points the way to repentance and faith in a new relationship—a relationship which is with God through Christ.

Thus, he is led to face clearly and with understanding that his relationship with God is one of separation because of personal sin and of his need of experiencing the new birth. Faced with responsible choice, he accepts or rejects the salvation which is in Christ. If he accepts the salvation offered by Christ, then baptism is administered as the identification symbol of union with Christ. The Lord's Supper as symbolic of a *new* covenant meal is offered.

Still another approach to the question of children and the churches is that presented by L. Craig Ratliff in his doctoral dissertation at Southern Baptist Seminary.

In the thesis Dr. Ratliff affirms the following to be true to the teachings of the biblical revelation:

1. To be a Christian is to accept Christ as Saviour and Lord. For Jesus to be Saviour, he must be Lord, which is the rule of God in one's life. The rule of God through Jesus Christ is the cardinal concept in the teachings of Jesus.

2. Baptist churches have, historically, believed that only disciples of Jesus are to be members of Baptist churches. Thus a Baptist church is a group of disciples, gathered into a congregation, seeking as the body of Christ to do his will.

3. The child is not a condemned sinner prior to personal accountability. Evidence from the Scriptures as to the nature of God and his revelation to man would indicate that because of the history of the race, all persons are born with a tendency toward sin; all are destined to sin. However, the individual is not responsible for the sins of the race or his inherited nature. He becomes an actual sinner in the eyes of God when, as a morally responsible person, he chooses sin and re-

bels against God. Thus there is a time between birth and moral accountability when the child is not guilty for sin. Most Baptists would agree with Dr. W. T. Conner who affirmed original sin, denied original guilt, and taught that all dying where the conditions of personal responsibility to God were lacking were saved.

4. Each person becomes responsible for his eternal destiny when as a responsible person (time of accountability) he is confronted with the claims of Christ.

5. Most children prior to adolescence are not capable of becoming a disciple of Jesus according to the New Testament teaching of the meaning of discipleship. Or, early adolescence is the time when most children reach accountability.

6. Prior to the time of accountability, the child does have valid religious experiences befitting his age and development.

7. Through Christian nurture in the home and the church, the child is to be related to the church in a creative way as he is a catechumen (one who is being instructed, a learner) of the church.

Ratliff emphasizes that the religious experiences of children ought to be understood and cultivated as a natural and true expression of the child's religious nature. Such experiences affirm that the child not only is heard by God, he is acceptable to God just as he is. This is not to suggest the child will naturally and inevitably grow into becoming a Christian. It means that each child can and should be nurtured in the faith so as to have meaningful religious experiences.

Such an approach will clear away the three primary obstacles between the churches and their children. First, the stigma of original guilt, which has resulted in various types of heresies, is removed from the child. Second, churches and parents are relieved of the pressure for an early and perhaps spurious evangelism. That is, if parents believe their child to be damned, they will do everything to get the child saved.

Third, the acceptance of the religious experiences of childhood will allow a child to mature normally without adults reading too much into those experiences. When a little child says, "I love Jesus and want to go to heaven," it should be accepted at face value. It is a sincere response on his own level in the quest for the fulfilment of the divine image. Tragedy often results when parents, teachers, and pastors read into such statements their own religious experience. This is to do violence to the very nature of a child.

Conclusion

The total picture before us should make clear the fact that there is no way to offer any simple, clear-cut, or automatic solutions to the problems which we are facing. A major factor which complicates the difficulties which we encounter is the fact that Southern Baptist churches are a part of the culture of this nation. The psychology of the United States is largely a pragmatic one based upon "growth," "success," and "achievement"; so the churches themselves are caught up in the obsession for growth, success, and achievement. So to a far higher degree than we like to admit, we are caught up in the deadly snare of statistics.

One result of this situation is that churches, pastors, and particularly evangelists are judged almost completely upon the basis of the number added to the church rolls. This results in the exercise of intense pressures at such times as Vacation Bible School decision services and evangelistic meetings. The preacher seems impelled by the setting in which he works to get people to "come forward."

As churches major less and less on an evangelistic outreach to adults and young people in the surrounding communities, they turn more and more to the children of the adults who are already church members because those children are the most readily accessible means of increasing the church rolls.

One must not think, however, that preachers are the only ones caught up in this philosophy. The actions of pulpit committees often reflect it to an equally high degree. During the past nineteen years the writer has served as interim pastor in twenty Baptist churches. He has found that in the discussions of the pulpit committees of these churches the primary criterion for an acceptable pastor was often the number of additions to the church of which he was currently pastor. In the first meeting of one pulpit committee a member said, "All we need to do is to get copies of associational minutes and go down the list of pastors and churches. The church which reports the largest number of additions is the pastor we want."

"Tragic," you say! Yes, but all too true. Such attitudes and practices did not come about suddenly but are the result of many factors operating over a long period of time and involving all of us both individually and collectively. Therefore, the primary fact which we must face as a denomination is that together we must engage in a process of a reexamination of our theology and practice concerning children and the church.

The practical outworking of such an examination ought to be seen in: (1) our goals—what we are really trying to achieve in the lives of our children; (2) our methods—in both evangelism and education— how realistically are they adapted to the true situation of the growth and development of the total person, the demands of biblical faith, and to facing and living of life in our time. The goals we set and the methods we use must be subject constantly to the central biblical concepts of the nature of mankind and his relation to God.

In chapter 2 the author shows that an understanding of the nature of man is basic to a development of a theology of children and the church. This is vital since the modern world is inclined to regard man as the evolutionary product of natural processes (naturalism), as being his own God in an autonomous world (secular humanism). Therefore the world tends to regard man as a being who is completely free to choose his own existence, since there is no God and the only reality is the here and now (atheistic existentialism).

While the biblical writers knew nothing of modern psychology and psychiatry, they did offer an understanding of man which is eternally significant and contemporary. This understanding may be summed up in four steps:

1. *Man is made in God's image.*—This means that the child is born with the potential of responding to God, having in himself some of the qualities of his creator, and reflecting back to God something of God's glory. It means that each person is a unified being and the physical and spiritual are but two aspects of this unity. It means that every person is made to live in responsible relationship with God and others. It means that man carries eternity in his heart, and if he does not worship Jehovah God, then he will worship a God of his own making. It means that man attains true personhood only within the structure of human relationships. It means that man is to subdue (understand, conquer) the earth so that the divine image in himself may reflect God's glory.

2. *The Bible reveals man also as a sinner in need of redemption.* —The story in the third chapter of Genesis reveals that the essence of sin is the conclusion that man can be self-secure and independent of God, that man can even be God. Because of the feelings of insecurity growing out of his limitations as a creature and because of the pride

growing out of his newly discovered powers, man chose to make himself independent of God, trying to be equal with God. Thus he became a creature of bondage. The story of the Garden of Eden is a true portrayal of every person. We all begin in the Garden with a dawning of self-consciousness; then we begin to act in rebellion against our rightful ruler, thereby selling ourselves into the bondage of sin.

3. *The heart of the gospel is that man's alienation and lostness can only be overcome in God's action in Christ (2 Cor. 5:19).*—Christ died for all. Potentially, all persons in all places have been redeemed in him. But—redemption becomes actual only as each person commits himself in faith to God as revealed in Jesus Christ.

4. *Man truly becomes man in Christ.*—This is the new humanity. The New Testament teaches that a Christian is one in whom Christ is forming himself again, so that the Christian grows toward the final consummation beyond death when he shall be made complete in the risen Lord.

These essential truths provide the biblical framework for our efforts with all men. Our work with children, therefore, will be biblical only to the degree that we are faithful to these concepts.

Contributors

George R. Beasley-Murray, principal, Spurgeon's College, London.
B.D. London University (Spurgeon's College) 1941; M.Th. London
(King's College) 1945; M.A. Cambridge (Jesus College) 1950; Ph.D
London (King's College) 1952; D.D. London, 1963. Pastor in London
and in Cambridge, 1941-50; lecturer in Greek New Testament Language
and Literature, Spurgeon's College, 1950; professor of Greek New Testament, Baptist Theological Seminary, Rüschlikon, Switzerland, 1956;
principal, Spurgeon's College, London, 1958.

William B. Coble, professor of New Testament Interpretation and
Greek, Midwestern Baptist Theological Seminary. B.A., Howard Payne
College, 1943; Th.M., Southwestern Baptist Theological Seminary, 1946;
Th.D., Southwestern Baptist Theological Seminary, 1956; postgraduate
study, University of Chicago Divinity School and Garrett Theological
Seminary, 1967-68; professor, Baptist Chair of Bible, and director of
Baptist Student Union, Stephen F. Austin State College, 1948-53; pro-
fessor, Baptist Chair of Bible, North Texas State University, 1953-60;
pastoral experience, six years; member, American Academy of Religion,
Society of Biblical Literature; Midwestern Baptist Theological Seminary,
1960.

William L. Hendricks, professor of Theology, Southwestern Baptist
Theological Seminary. A.B., Oklahoma Baptist University, 1951; B.D.,
Southwestern Baptist Theological Seminary, 1954; Th.D. Southwestern
Baptist Theological Seminary, 1958; M.A., University of Chicago, 1965;
additional study at the University of Chicago, 1964-65; Union Seminary;
Southern Methodist University; Texas Christian University; pastorates,
Golden Acres Baptist Mission, Shawnee, Oklahoma; South Baptist Church,

Dodson, Texas; assistant pastor, Immanuel Baptist Church, Wichita, Kansas; counselor of boys, Buckner Orphans Home, Dallas, Texas; member, Society of Biblical Literature, American Academy of Religion; contributor to *Teacher's Quarterly, Baptist Student, Window, Training Union Magazine.*

Roy L. Honeycutt, Jr., professor of Old Testament Interpretation and Hebrew, Midwestern Baptist Theological Seminary, B.A., Mississippi College, 1950; B.D., Southern Baptist Theological Seminary, 1952; Th.D., Southern Baptist Theological Seminary, 1958; postgraduate study, University of Edinburgh, Scotland, 1966-67; fellow and instructor, Southern Baptist Theological Seminary, 1952-57; pastoral experience, eleven years; U.S. Army 1944-46, Pacific Theater; associate member, Society for Old Testament Study, Great Britain; member, American Academy of Religion, Society of Biblical Literature, American Schools of Oriental Research, Association of Baptist Professors of Religion; author, *Amos and His Message* (Broadman), *Amos: Study Guide for Seminary Extension, Crisis and Response* (Abingdon), *These Ten Words* (Broadman), Sunday School lesson materials; contributor, *Review and Expositor, Foundations, Southwestern Journal of Theology,* denominational papers; Midwestern Baptist Theological Seminary, 1959.

Clifford Ingle, professor of Church Administration and Religious Education, Midwestern Baptist Theological Seminary. A.A., Southwest Baptist College, 1936; A.B., William Jewell College, 1938; B.D., Southwestern Baptist Theological Seminary, 1947; M.R.E., Southwestern Baptist Theological Seminary, 1948; D.R.E., Southwestern Baptist Theological Seminary, 1952; postgraduate study, University of Chicago Divinity School and Lutheran Theological Seminary of Chicago, 1967-68; fellow, Southwestern Baptist Theological Seminary, 1949-51; teacher-director, Baptist Student Center, Springfield, Mo., 1951-59; professor, Philosophy and Ethics, Southwest Missouri State College, 1957-59; pastoral experience, fifteen years; chaplain, U.S. Army, Pacific and European Theaters, 1942-46; author, *The Military Chaplain as a Counselor, a New Commitment;* member, Southwestern Baptist Religious Education Association, National Religious Education Association, American Academy of Religion, Association of Seminary Professors in the Practical Fields; Midwestern Baptist Theological Seminary, 1959.

E. Paul Torrance, chairman and professor, Department of Educational Psychology, University of Georgia. A.B., Mercer University, 1940; M.A., University of Minnesota, 1944; Ph.D., University of Michigan, 1951; teacher, counselor, principal, Georgia Military College, 1937-44; psychologist and psychiatric social worker, U.S. Disciplinary Barracks, U.S. Army, 1945-46; counselor and associate professor of Psychology, Kansas State University, 1946-48; director, Counseling Bureau, and professor of

Psychology, Kansas State University, 1949-51; director of research, Survival Research Field Unit, Air Force Personnel and Training Research Center, 1951-57; director, Bureau of Educational Research, University of Minnesota, 1958-64; professor of Educational Psychology, University of Minnesota, 1964-66; chairman and professor, Department of Educational Psychology, University of Georgia, 1966 to present. fellow, Division of Educational Psychology, American Psychological Association; member, Committee on the Practice of Psychology in the Schools; American Educational Research Association; The Religious Education Association; author, books on creativity, mental health, and stress.

Hugh Wamble, professor of Church History, Midwestern Baptist Theological Seminary. A.B., Mercer University, 1949; A.M., University of Missouri, 1966; B.D., Southern Baptist Theological Seminary, 1951; Th.D., Southern Baptist Theological Seminary, 1956; postgraduate study, Duke University, 1958-59; instructor, Southern Baptist Theological Seminary, 1955-56; assistant professor of Church History, Southern Baptist Theological Seminary, 1956-58; pastoral experience, 1951-55; U.S. Marine Corps, 1942-45; author, *Through Trial to Triumph, The Shape of Faith, A History of Christian Thought* (for Seminary Extension); contributor, *Encyclopedia of Southern Baptists, Review and Expositor, The Quarterly Review, Foundations, Church History, Missouri Historical Review,* and other periodicals; member American Society of Church History, American Historical Association; Midwestern Baptist Theological Seminary, 1959.